MILITARY PAY AND BENEFITS

COSTS AND CONSIDERATIONS

MILITARY AND VETERAN ISSUES

Additional books in this series can be found on Nova's website
under the Series tab.

Additional E-books in this series can be found on Nova's website
under the E-book tab.

MILITARY AND VETERAN ISSUES

MILITARY PAY AND BENEFITS

COSTS AND CONSIDERATIONS

WALTER AVRAHAM
EDITOR

nova publishers

New York

Copyright © 2013 by Nova Science Publishers, Inc.

For permission to use material from this book please contact us:
Telephone 631-231-7269; Fax 631-231-8175
Web Site: http://www.novapublishers.com

NOTICE TO THE READER

The Publisher has taken reasonable care in the preparation of this book, but makes no expressed or implied warranty of any kind and assumes no responsibility for any errors or omissions. No liability is assumed for incidental or consequential damages in connection with or arising out of information contained in this book. The Publisher shall not be liable for any special, consequential, or exemplary damages resulting, in whole or in part, from the readers' use of, or reliance upon, this material. Any parts of this book based on government reports are so indicated and copyright is claimed for those parts to the extent applicable to compilations of such works.

Independent verification should be sought for any data, advice or recommendations contained in this book. In addition, no responsibility is assumed by the publisher for any injury and/or damage to persons or property arising from any methods, products, instructions, ideas or otherwise contained in this publication.

This publication is designed to provide accurate and authoritative information with regard to the subject matter covered herein. It is sold with the clear understanding that the Publisher is not engaged in rendering legal or any other professional services. If legal or any other expert assistance is required, the services of a competent person should be sought. FROM A DECLARATION OF PARTICIPANTS JOINTLY ADOPTED BY A COMMITTEE OF THE AMERICAN BAR ASSOCIATION AND A COMMITTEE OF PUBLISHERS.

Additional color graphics may be available in the e-book version of this book.

Library of Congress Cataloging-in-Publication Data

ISBN: 978-1-62417-809-2

Published by Nova Science Publishers, Inc. † New York

CONTENTS

PREFACE

From the earliest days of the republic, America's Armed Forces have been compensated by military pay, commonly known as "basic pay." While the original pay structure was quite simple and straightforward, over time a complex system of pay, allowances, incentives, and bonuses has evolved. With the advent of the all-volunteer force in 1973, Congress has used military pay and its associated allowances to improve recruiting, retention, and the overall quality of the force. This book addresses the role of military pay in manning the Armed Forces, the types of pay increases used in the past, recent reforms in managing pay, and the role of the Employment Cost Index in determining pay increases.

Chapter 1 – Compensation of military personnel takes up a substantial portion of the nation's defense budget. In its fiscal year 2013 budget request, for example, the Department of Defense (DoD) requested about $150 billion to fund the pay and benefits of current and retired members of the armed services. As in most recent years, that amount was more than one-quarter of DoD's total base budget request (the request for all funding other than for military operations in Iraq and Afghanistan and for related activities—often called overseas contingency operations). The compensation request involved four major areas:

- Current cash compensation for service members, consisting of basic pay, food and housing allowances, bonuses, and various types of special pay;
- Accrual payments that account for the future cash compensation of current service members in the form of pensions for those who will retire from the military (generally after at least 20 years of service);

- Accrual payments that account for the future costs of health care for current service members (under a program called TRICARE for Life) who will retire from the military and also become eligible for Medicare (generally at age 65); and
- Funding for current spending under the military health care program (known as TRICARE), excluding the costs of caring for current military retirees who also are eligible for Medicare (the latter costs are covered by the accrual payments made in earlier years, just described).

In all, about 1.4 million active-duty military personnel and about 1.1 million members of the reserves and National Guard receive current cash compensation, the largest part of compensation in DoD's budget. Cash compensation for members of the reserves and National Guard goes mainly to the 840,000 members of the Selected Reserve—service members who are assigned to and train regularly with standing units. Second in total cost to current cash compensation, military health benefits are available to nearly 10 million people: active-duty military personnel and their eligible family members, retired military personnel and their eligible family members, survivors of service members who died while on active duty, and certain members of the reserves and National Guard.

This report does not consider the costs of the benefits provided by the Department of Veterans Affairs (VA)— about $130 billion in that department's 2013 budget request. Those benefits include health care for veterans with service-connected disabilities and for veterans who meet certain other eligibility criteria. Other VA benefits include monthly cash payments that compensate for service-connected disabilities and GI Bill benefits that reimburse some of the costs of higher education.

This report also does not consider the costs of pay and benefits for DoD's roughly 790,000 full-time-equivalent civilian employees, other than for the 60,000 who are assigned to the military health care system and whose compensation contributes to the estimate of the total cost of delivering military health care.

Chapter 2 – From the earliest days of the republic, America's Armed Forces have been compensated by military pay, commonly known as "basic pay." While the original pay structure was quite simple and straightforward, over time a complex system of pay, allowances, incentives, and bonuses has evolved.

With the advent of the all-volunteer force in 1973, Congress has used military pay and its associated allowances to improve recruiting, retention, and the overall quality of the force. Congress, in the National Defense Authorization Act, typically authorizes military pay adjustments for the coming fiscal year. Today's ongoing military operations in Iraq and Afghanistan, combined with concern over government spending and the debt ceiling, suggest that further changes in pay, allowances, incentives, and bonuses will continue to receive congressional scrutiny.

In the nearly 10 years since the terrorist attacks of September 11, 2001, basic pay has increased nominally by nearly 35% (figure not adjusted for inflation). This figure does not include other increases in allowances, bonuses, or incentives. The cumulative effect is that most analysts now agree that the average annual cost per servicemember exceeds $100,000.

Many observers are currently concerned about the cost of recent manpower increases, the impact of personnel costs on the overall defense budget, and the potential decrement to equipment modernization plans caused by the increased pressure of the personnel account. To date, however, it appears that the increasing cost of personnel has not come at the expense of other elements in the defense budget.

The issue of pay comparability between military and civilian pay, commonly referred to as the "pay gap," continues to receive emphasis. Advocates for higher pay have emphasized the sacrifices being made today by the American military, the high personnel tempo and reduced dwell time, the impact on families caused by frequent deployments, and the positive impact that raises have had on recruiting and retention. Others argue that the "pay gap" is an imprecise measurement that does not fully account for other compensation increases in the form of allowances, incentives, and bonuses. Still others believe that the military is already better compensated than their civilian counterparts, especially during this period of high unemployment.

The Department of Defense (DOD), on the other hand, bases its recommendations regarding military pay on its own standard for pay comparability. The DOD standard establishes that members should be compensated at the 70th percentile of wages for civilian employees with similar levels of education, age, experience, and responsibility.

This report addresses the role of military pay in manning the Armed Forces, the types of pay increases used in the past, recent reforms in managing pay, and the role of the Employment Cost Index in determining basic pay increases. The report also reviews the compensation benefits specifically available to military personnel participating in Operation Iraqi Freedom (OIF)/Operation New Dawn (OND) and Operation Enduring Freedom (OEF).

Chapter 3 – The Department of Defense (DOD) spent about $5.6 billion in fiscal year 2010 on special and incentive pays and bonuses for active-duty servicemembers. Of that amount, about $1.2 billion was contracted for enlistment and reenlistment bonuses. DOD uses these incentives and bonuses as tools in its compensation system to help ensure that military pay is sufficient to field a high-quality, all-volunteer force, including those in hard-to-fill or critical specialties. Special pays and bonuses comprise about 5 percent of DOD's budget for cash compensation and less than 1 percent of its overall budget. In addition to cash compensation, which includes bonuses and basic pay, the department provides active-duty personnel with a comprehensive compensation package that includes noncash benefits, such as health care, and deferred compensation, such as retirement pensions.

In 2005, we recommended that DOD assess its compensation system's effectiveness, including an analysis of the reasonableness and appropriateness of its allocation of cash and benefits. DOD agreed with our recommendation, stating that it was already engaged in multiple efforts to assess its compensation strategy. Subsequently, the Senate report to accompany a bill for the National Defense Authorization Act for Fiscal Year 2011 (S. 3454) directed GAO to assess DOD's and the services' use of cash incentives to recruit and retain highly qualified individuals for service in the armed forces to fill hard-to-fill or critical wartime specialties and review the extent to which the services have an effective process for designating an occupation as critical or hard-to-fill. Effective management of cash incentives is particularly important, given the current budgetary environment and the Secretary of Defense's initiatives to instill a culture of savings and cost accountability across DOD. Moreover, the Secretary of Defense has acknowledged and expressed concern about growing personnel costs crowding out DOD's ability to spend on its other needs. Accordingly, this report (1) identifies recent trends in the services' use of enlistment and reenlistment bonuses, (2) assesses the extent to which the services have processes that enable them to determine which occupational specialties should be offered bonuses and whether bonus amounts are optimally set, and (3) determines how much flexibility DOD has in managing selected special and incentive pays for officer and enlisted personnel.

To determine the recent trends in the use of enlistment and reenlistment bonuses, we analyzed service data on contracted enlistment and reenlistment bonuses for fiscal years 2006 through 2010. To evaluate the extent to which the services have processes to designate occupations that should be offered bonuses and whether bonus amounts are optimally set, we reviewed DOD and service regulations pertaining to their processes for designating bonus-eligible occupations. We also interviewed relevant DOD and service officials with responsibilities for designating occupations as bonus eligible and obtained information on analytical tools such as statistical models used by the services to identify bonus-eligible occupations. To determine how much flexibility DOD has in managing selected special and incentive pays, we analyzed data on 15 special and incentive pays across the services for fiscal years 2006 through 2010, which represented the top five expenditures for special and incentive pays each year for each service. We focused on pays that were available to most servicemembers. For this reason, we excluded medical pays. We conducted this performance audit from September 2010 through June 2011 in accordance with generally accepted government auditing standards. These standards require that we plan and perform the audit to obtain sufficient, appropriate evidence to provide a reasonable basis for our findings and conclusions based on our research objectives. We believe that the evidence obtained provides a reasonable basis for our findings and conclusions based on our audit objectives. (See app. I for further details on our scope and methodology.)

Chapter 4 – This is the Statement of Carla Tighe Murray, Senior Analyst for Military Compensation and Health Care, Congressional Budget Office. Hearing on "Military Compensation and Benefits."

In: Military Pay and Benefits
Editor: Walter Avraham

ISBN: 978-1-62417-809-2
© 2013 Nova Science Publishers, Inc.

Chapter 1

COSTS OF MILITARY PAY AND BENEFITS IN THE DEFENSE BUDGET[*]

Matthew S. Goldberg

NOTES

Unless otherwise indicated, all years referred to in this study are federal fiscal years (which run from October 1 to September 30). Numbers in the text and tables may not add up to totals because of rounding. On the cover: A member of the U.S. Marine Corps in Afghanistan records information before disbursing pay (photo by U.S. Marine Corps Lance Corporal Khoa Pelczar). On pages 3 and 22, CBO's estimate of the cumulative decline in military basic pay (under the Department of Defense's plan for the 2013—2017 period) relative to projected growth in the employment cost index has been revised from what was published originally to correct an error in calculation.

SUMMARY

Compensation of military personnel takes up a substantial portion of the nation's defense budget. In its fiscal year 2013 budget request, for example,

---

[*] This is an edited, reformatted and augmented version of Congressional Budget Office report, Publication No. 4234, dated November 2012.

the Department of Defense (DoD) requested about $150 billion to fund the pay and benefits of current and retired members of the armed services. As in most recent years, that amount was more than one-quarter of DoD's total base budget request (the request for all funding other than for military operations in Iraq and Afghanistan and for related activities—often called overseas contingency operations). The compensation request involved four major areas:

- Current cash compensation for service members, consisting of basic pay, food and housing allowances, bonuses, and various types of special pay;
- Accrual payments that account for the future cash compensation of current service members in the form of pensions for those who will retire from the military (generally after at least 20 years of service);
- Accrual payments that account for the future costs of health care for current service members (under a program called TRICARE for Life) who will retire from the military and also become eligible for Medicare (generally at age 65); and
- Funding for current spending under the military health care program (known as TRICARE), excluding the costs of caring for current military retirees who also are eligible for Medicare (the latter costs are covered by the accrual payments made in earlier years, just described).

In all, about 1.4 million active-duty military personnel and about 1.1 million members of the reserves and National Guard receive current cash compensation, the largest part of compensation in DoD's budget. Cash compensation for members of the reserves and National Guard goes mainly to the 840,000 members of the Selected Reserve—service members who are assigned to and train regularly with standing units. Second in total cost to current cash compensation, military health benefits are available to nearly 10 million people: active-duty military personnel and their eligible family members, retired military personnel and their eligible family members, survivors of service members who died while on active duty, and certain members of the reserves and National Guard.

This report does not consider the costs of the benefits provided by the Department of Veterans Affairs (VA)— about $130 billion in that department's 2013 budget request. Those benefits include health care for veterans with service-connected disabilities and for veterans who meet certain other eligibility criteria. Other VA benefits include monthly cash payments that compensate for service-connected disabilities and GI Bill benefits that reimburse some of the costs of higher education.

This report also does not consider the costs of pay and benefits for DoD's roughly 790,000 full-time-equivalent civilian employees, other than for the 60,000 who are assigned to the military health care system and whose compensation contributes to the estimate of the total cost of delivering military health care.

Projected Costs

Over the past decade, the costs per active-duty service member that are funded through DoD's military personnel account (which funds current cash compensation and the accrual payments for retirees' pensions and some of their health care) and the total costs for the military health care program have increased consistently, even with an adjustment for inflation in the general economy (see Summary Figure 1). The trend in the military personnel account is attributable primarily to a series of pay raises that exceeded the general rate of inflation and, in some years, the growth rate of private-sector wages and salaries.

In particular, the annual changes in basic military pay— the largest and most visible part of cash compensation— have since 2000 been linked to changes in the Bureau of Labor Statistics' employment cost index (ECI) for wages and salaries in private industry. The ECI historically has increased faster than prices, which are measured here using the deflator for gross domestic product (GDP). Moreover, in 2008, 2009, and 2010, lawmakers authorized military pay raises that were 0.5 percentage points above the increase in the ECI. Also at work in pushing up compensation costs were several enhancements to pension and health benefits for retired military personnel and medical costs per beneficiary that escalated more rapidly than did either general inflation or increases in per capita costs for medical care in the national economy.

DoD's plans, as reflected in the 2013 Future Years Defense Program (FYDP) submitted to the Congress in April 2012, do not include military pay raises that keep pace with the ECI from 2013 through 2017. Instead, the department's plans include a 1.7 percent pay raise for 2013. For 2014, DoD again proposes a raise of 1.7 percent, which is below the amount projected by the Congressional Budget Office (CBO) for the increase in the ECI for that year but is perhaps consistent with DoD's own projection of the ECI. For 2015 through 2017, DoD is proposing pay raises of 0.5 percent, 1.0 percent, and 1.5 percent, respectively—all smaller than the department's projection of ECI growth for those years. With those raises, basic pay would remain essentially flat in real (inflation-adjusted) terms (relative to the GDP deflator) between 2013 and 2017, and it would lose a total of 11 percentage points of growth relative to CBO's projection of the ECI for that period.

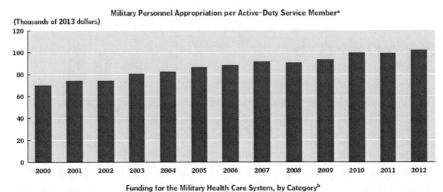

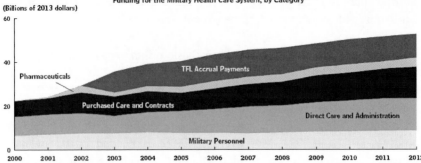

Source: Congressional Budget Office based on data contained in *Long-Term Implications of the 2013 Future Years Defense Program* (July 2012).

Note: Excludes funding for overseas contingency operations.

[a] Active-duty service members are counted as of the final day (September 30) of each fiscal year.

[b] The TRICARE for Life (TFL) program began in 2002 but was not funded on an accrual basis until 2003. Before 2001, pharmaceutical costs were not separately identifiable but were included in the costs of two categories: Purchased Care and Contracts and Direct Care and Administration. An initiative to separately identify pharmaceutical costs began in 2001, and since 2002, most pharmaceutical costs have been so identified. However, some of those costs incurred since 2003 have been included in the category TFL Accrual Payments.

Summary Figure 1. Funding for Military Compensation.

On the basis of DoD's 2013 FYDP, CBO projected that the costs of military health care that are funded by the accounts for military personnel and for operation and maintenance would rise from $51 billion in 2013 to $65 billion by 2017 and to $77 billion by 2022 (all measured in 2013 dollars).[1] Real growth in health care costs over the decade would average 4.6 percent per year, according to CBO's projections.

DoD's fiscal situation has changed as a result of the enactment of the Budget Control Act of 2011 (BCA, Public Law 112-25). To comply with that act, the Consolidated Appropriations Act, 2012 (P.L. 112-74), provided $530 billion for DoD's base budget—about $24 billion, or 4 percent, less than the department requested. CBO estimates that funding for fiscal year 2013 could drop to $469 billion—a cut of an additional 12 percent—if all of the BCA's provisions, including sequestration (the automatic cancellation of a portion of budgetary resources), remain in force. Even if the defense budget was cut by that amount, however, the costs of military compensation probably would not decline by the same percentage. Unless current law is changed, basic pay will continue to be linked to the ECI, and military health care costs will continue to grow rapidly. Thus, to comply with the BCA, DoD might have to take such steps as reducing the number of military personnel or cutting elements of compensation that are not automatically linked to the ECI or to other external economic indicators.

Controlling Costs

Several approaches could be taken to curtail spending on military compensation. One possibility would be to restrict basic pay raises, as DoD has proposed for 2015 through 2017. Although smaller raises could lead to fewer enlistments and faster attrition from the armed services, those consequences might be mitigated by increasing the availability of enlistment bonuses and selective reenlistment bonuses (the latter are offered to service members in hard-to-fill occupations). Reenlistment bonuses can be a useful tool for increasing retention while curbing costs because, in contrast to basic pay raises, they do not compound from year to year and they have no effect on the value of future retirement annuities.

Another approach to controlling compensation costs might be to replace the current retirement system (under which active-duty members qualify for immediate benefits after 20 years of service) with a defined-benefit system that partially vests earlier in a member's career or with a defined-contribution system under which DoD matches the service members' contributions to a savings plan or with some combination of the two systems. Those measures could cost less or more than the current system, depending on their structure and implementation. Any reductions in overall federal outlays stemming from new rules would be delayed for 20 years if all current service members remained in the current system. However, DoD could immediately begin to spend less on the accrual payments it makes to the Military Retirement Fund if the defined-benefit plan became, on balance, less generous.

Still another way to control compensation costs would be to increase health care enrollment fees, deductibles, or copayments. Higher enrollment fees raise collections by DoD and could discourage some retiree families from relying on DoD to provide their health care (thus generating further savings); higher deductibles and copayments also act to restrain the use of medical services and thereby reduce the government's cost. As an example, in the past CBO has examined an option that would preclude military retirees who are not yet eligible for Medicare from enrolling their families in TRICARE Prime (the TRICARE option that operates like a health maintenance organization), allowing them instead to pay to enroll in a plan that would provide access to a combination of network providers (similar to a preferred provider organization) and non-network providers (similar to a fee-for-service plan). CBO estimated that such an option could save the government as much as $10 billion per year.[2]

INTRODUCTION

The basic pay that all military service members receive is the largest and most visible component of military compensation, and, in many recent years, annual adjustments in basic pay have been a source of contention between the Administration and the Congress. Despite that, however, basic pay accounts for only about one-third of all military compensation. The Department of Defense (DoD) relies on a complex system of current and deferred, cash and noncash compensation to attract and retain service members (see Table 1). In some areas, DoD has considerable flexibility to adjust compensation in what it deems the most effective way to attract and retain service members; in other areas, current law limits that flexibility. In all cases, current law provides the authority for DoD to structure its compensation system.

To aid the Congress in its consideration of the military compensation system, this study examines a range of issues from two perspectives: that of the service members and retirees who are compensated by the system and that of the DoD budget. Each point of view is important for elucidating the way the compensation system is operated, how much it costs, and how it affects those who receive the compensation.

Defining Military Compensation: The Service Member's Perspective

DoD measures the largest elements of current cash compensation that all service members regularly receive by means of a construct called regular military compensation (RMC): basic pay plus allowances for subsistence (food) and housing and an estimate of the financial advantage that arises because those allowances are not subject to federal income taxes.

The basic pay component varies with a member's pay grade and years of service. Subsistence allowances are paid at one monthly rate for enlisted personnel and another for officers, and housing allowances depend not just on pay grade but also on location and whether a member has dependents. Thus, in calendar year 2012, an enlisted member in the fourth-most-junior pay grade (E-4 or, in the Army, corporal) with between 48 months and 72 months of service earns annual basic pay of $27,200 and a subsistence allowance of $4,180. Housing allowances vary considerably by location, but the average for a member with dependents stationed in the continental United States is $14,820.[1] With an estimated tax advantage of $4,660, that service member's RMC for the year comes to $50,860. An officer in the third-most-junior rank (an Army captain or a Navy lieutenant with a pay grade of O-3) with six years of service and at least one dependent earns basic pay of $63,260; the current RMC for that service member is $92,220.[2]

In addition to RMC, some service members receive other forms of current cash compensation at various points or, in some cases, throughout their careers:

- Enlistment, reenlistment, and officer accession and retention bonuses;
- Special or incentive pay for service members (such as physicians, nuclear-qualified technicians, and aviators) who acquire or retain critical skills or for those who improve proficiency (such as doctors who achieve board certification or aviators who log additional operational flying time); and

- Pay for accepting difficult or dangerous assignments, such as assignment incentive pay, special duty pay, hostile fire or imminent danger pay, and family separation allowances.

For fiscal year 2013, DoD requested $51 billion for basic pay and $7 billion for all of those forms of special and incentive pay. Current noncash compensation includes benefits that service members can use immediately, including health care for themselves and their eligible family members, subsidies for groceries and consumer goods sold at military commissaries and exchanges, use of recreation centers, and subsidized child care. eferred compensation includes both cash compensation in the form of military retirement annuities and noncash benefits such as health care for retirees and their eligible family members and continued access to the commissaries and exchanges. Other deferred benefits, funded through the Department of Veterans Affairs (VA) rather than through DoD, include access to health care and other benefits such as monthly cash payments for service-connected disabilities and GI Bill benefits that reimburse some of the costs of higher education.

Table 1. Types of Military Compensation

Cash	Noncash[a]
	Current
• Basic pay	• Health care for service member and family
• Housing allowance	• Subsidized groceries at commissaries
• Subsistence (Food) allowance	• Subsidized consumer goods at exchanges
• Bonuses and special pay	• Subsidized child care
	• Fitness and recreation centers
	• Deployment support programs for military families
	Deferred
• Military retirement pay (Pension)	• Health care for retired service member and family
	• Subsidized groceries at commissaries
	• Subsidized consumer goods at exchanges

Source: Congressional Budget Office.
a. The items shown are the major categories of noncash compensation.

Current noncash and deferred compensation is more difficult to measure than is current cash compensation, but at least three measurement concepts are of potential interest:

- The costs borne by DoD (and possibly other federal agencies) to provide a given benefit;
- The value of the benefit as perceived by service members, conceptually measured as the amount of current cash compensati on a service member would be willing to accept in lieu of the benefit; or
- The savings to a beneficiary, conceptually measured as what the beneficiary would spend (for example, on out-of-pocket charges for health care) if the goods or services were not provided by the military.[3]

This report focuses on the first of those three concepts — the costs borne by DoD.[4]

Defining Military Compensation: The Budgetary Perspective

About 1.4 million people serve on active duty in the military, and another 1.1 million are in the reserves and National Guard. Compensation costs for the latter two groups are principally for the 840,000 members of the Selected Reserve, who are assigned to and regularly train with standing units.

In all, nearly 10 million people are eligible for health care benefits provided through TRICARE (the military health care program) and TRICARE for Life (TFL, the supplementary health care program for retired service members and their dependents who also are eligible for Medicare).

Those beneficiaries include all active-duty service members and their eligible family members, retired military personnel and their eligible family members, survivors of service members who died while on active duty, and certain members of the reserves and National Guard. Researchers, policymakers, and others define military compensation in various ways, and no single definition is universally accepted.

The Congressional Budget Office (CBO) developed the definitions used in this study with reference to the organization of DoD's budget, which is divided generally into six large categories: military personnel (MILPERS); operation and maintenance (O&M); research, development, test, and evaluation (RDT&E); procurement; military construction; and family housing. This study defines funding for military compensation as the sum of four parts:

- The MILPERS appropriation for pay, bonuses, and allowances;
- Accrual payments into the Military Retirement Fund, which account for future cash compensation in the form of pensions for the subset of current service members who eventually will retire from the military (generally after at least 20 years of service);

Table 2. DoD's Funding Request for Military Compensation, 2013

	Billions of Dollars
Military Personnel Appropriation	
Basic pay	51.2
Other pay and allowances	37.5
Accrual payments into the Military Retirement Fund	16.4
Accrual payments into the MERHCF	6.7
Transfer of personnel costs from the OCO budget[a]	5.3
Subtotal[b]	117.0
Defense Health Program, Operation and Maintenance Appropriation	
Direct care at military medical treatment facilities and administrative costs[c]	14.1
Purchased care and contracts	14.2
Pharmaceuticals	3.8
Subtotal[d]	32.0
Total	149.0

Source: Congressional Budget Office.
Notes: All entries are for the base budget only and exclude additional funding requested for overseas contingency operations.
DoD = Department of Defense; MERHCF = Medicare-Eligible Retiree Health Care Fund; OCO = overseas contingency operations.
[a] CBO transferred into the base budget the personnel costs for the 41,000 soldiers and 15,000 marines on active duty whom DoD is planning to pay from the OCO budget.
[b] Excludes $4.6 billion for permanent change-of-station travel and $18.8 billion for other activities requested in the military personnel appropriation.
[c] Excludes $8.2 billion in the military personnel appropriation for the pay and allowances of 86,000 military medical personnel who provide health care at military treatment facilities; that amount is included in the subtotal for the military personnel appropriation.
[d] Excludes $0.5 billion for procurement and $0.7 billion for research, development, test, and evaluation in the budget request for the Defense Health Program.

- Accrual payments into the Medicare-Eligible Retiree Health Care Fund (MERHCF), which account for the future costs of health care (under TFL) for the subset of current service members who eventually will retire from the military and also become eligible for Medicare (generally at age 65); and
- Funding from the O&M appropriation for TRICARE, excluding the costs of caring for current military retirees who also are eligible for Medicare (the latter costs are financed by outlays from the MERHCF, as described above).

Under the assumptions and definitions CBO has adopted for this report, DoD's 2013 request for military compensation was $149 billion, or 28 percent of its total base budget request of $526 billion (see Table 2). The largest share of military compensation comes from the MILPERS appropriation. Other activities that CBO classifies as compensation are funded from other appropriations. In particular, the O&M appropriation provides significant funding for military health care, with smaller amounts for health care coming from the procurement and RDT&E accounts. The MILPERS appropriation contains the funds for basic military pay, subsistence and housing allowances, all of the various types of special and incentive pay, bonuses, and the government's share (as the employer) of the social insurance taxes that fund Social Security and Medicare benefits. Some funds from the MILPERS appropriation are used to make accrual payments to account for the future pension costs for the current active-duty population; DoD estimates those payments at roughly one-third the value of active-duty basic pay. However, CBO excludes from its definition of military compensation the funds contained in the MILPERS account that pay moving expenses for service members and their families who relocate to new duty stations (about 3 percent of that account) and other costs that are borne by DoD but not reflected in service members' paychecks (for example, the costs of apprehending military deserters). Taking all of those elements of compensation together, the requested MILPERS appropriation for 2013 includes $117 billion for military compensation (see Table 2).

Another $32 billion that CBO classifies as military compensation was requested through the O&M appropriation.That part of the O&M budget supports the Defense Health Program.[5] Specifically, those funds support direct care at military medical treatment facilities and administrative costs, purchased health care and contracts for such care, and pharmaceuticals. The $8.2 billion cost of the pay and allowances for the 86,000 military personnel whom DoD plans to assign to the military health care system is included in the MILPERS appropriation. In 2013, DoD also budgeted $74 billion for the pay and benefits of about 790,000 full-time-equivalent civilian employees, mostly from the O&M appropriation but with smaller amounts coming from procurement and RDT&E funds. CBO does not consider those costs in this analysis of military compensation, except implicitly for the 60,000 civilian employees who are assigned to the military health care system and whose compensation is included in the O&M cost of delivering military health care. The definition of military compensation used in this report accounts for most, but not all, of the costs of military compensation in DoD's budget. It excludes such noncash benefits as fitness and recreation centers, subsidized child care, and subsidies for groceries sold at military commissaries; CBO's definition also excludes deployment support programs that provide various types of assistance to military families. (For additional discussion of noncash benefits, see Box 1.) The definition of military compensation used in this report also greatly understates the total amount that the federal government pays for current and former military personnel. The discussion here is restricted to DoD's budget and excludes VA benefits (see Box 2 on page 10). VA's funding request for 2013 includes $56 billion for its medical program and $76 billion for its other programs.[6] The total of $132 billion is nearly 90 percent of the amount ($149 billion) for military compensation that CBO identified in DoD's request for the same year. In addition, the definition of compensation used here excludes the tax revenues lost to the U.S. Treasury because subsistence and housing allowances are exempt from the federal income tax, as are many types of pay and bonuses if earned in a combat zone. Finally, because of the emphasis on DoD's budget, CBO's definition of military compensation also excludes accrual payments that the Treasury (not DoD) makes to fund "concurrent receipt"—the ability of some retired military personnel to receive military retirement pay without any offset for the VA compensation they receive for service-connected disabilities.[7]

Box 1. Subsidized Goods and In-Kind Compensation

The availability of noncash benefits—free health care and subsidized child care, for example—increases the attractiveness of military service as a career path. And the similarity from one base to another, even in remote locations or overseas, of goods and services to be found at commissaries, exchanges, and recreation facilities reduces costs and can temper the difficulty of changing schools, finding places to shop, and acquiring housing as service members move from place to place.

Some costs of noncash benefits are easy to estimate, such as the $1.4 billion annual appropriation to the Defense Commissary Agency that covers a portion of the agency's operating costs and, in effect, subsidizes its food sales. For other elements of compensation, such as access to fitness centers, it is conceptually difficult to separate a personal benefit—in this case, recreation—from the institutional benefit of promoting service members' readiness to perform a mission.

Other types of compensation, such as on-base parking, although undoubtedly valued by service members, are not accounted for separately in budget documents. For this study, rather than including only the subset of those benefits for which costs are most easily estimated, the Congressional Budget Office simply excluded all noncash benefits other than health care.

Some observers assert that a shift from paying service members in the form of subsidies and in-kind benefits toward providing more cash compensation would allow individual service members to purchase the goods and services they value most and help the department to retain service members for a longer term at a lower total cost.[1]

Moreover, because two-thirds of active-duty service members live off-base, as do all nonactivated reservists, on-base facilities may not serve those members as effectively as a more cash-based system might. Finally, it could be simpler for the department to direct cash incentives to the service members who are most productive or whose skills are of greatest value to the military for the long term.

1. Carla Tighe Murray, "Transforming In-Kind Compensation and Benefits," in Cindy Williams, ed. *Filling the Ranks: Transforming the U.S. Military Personnel System* (MIT Press, 2004).

MILITARY COMPENSATION IN THE CONTEXT OF THE DEFENSE BUDGET

The funding caps in the Budget Control Act of 2011 (BCA, Public Law 112-25) require significant cuts in DoD's budget relative to the budgetary plan expressed in the department's 2013 Future Years Defense Program (FYDP). If, as in the past, DoD continues to receive 95.5 percent of all funding in budget function 050 (national defense)—and before considering the additional reductions in funding caps that would stem from the BCA's automatic enforcement procedures—the department's base budget (net of funding for overseas contingency operations, or OCO) will decline by a total of $22 billion (in nominal dollars) relative to its five-year plan for 2013–2017. If, further, the automatic enforcement procedures are triggered in January 2013, DoD's base budget will drop by $52 billion more per year, CBO estimates, bringing the five-year cuts to a total of $282 billion, or 10 percent of the amount in DoD's plan.

By 2021—the final year explicitly addressed by the BCA—the reduced cap on DoD's budget would be 15 percent lower than the real (inflation-adjusted) amount appropriated for 2012.

(Box 3 on page 12 gives estimates of the trajectory for the defense budget under the terms of the BCA.) The scheduled reductions will be extremely difficult to achieve without reducing the number of military personnel, curtailing their pay and benefits, or undertaking some combination of those two actions.

DoD's Compensation Plans and Funding Under Current Law

DoD's 2013 FYDP contained a plan to decrease active-duty end strength (the number of military service personnel on the rolls as of the final day of a fiscal year) by 72,000, or about 5 percent, over five years—from 1,392,000 in 2013 to 1,320,000 by 2017.

To comply with the BCA's funding caps (before automatic enforcement procedures take effect), DoD's plan shifted the personnel costs for 41,000 soldiers and 15,000 marines on active duty from the base budget to the OCO budget in 2013 and made similar but smaller shifts for 2014 through 2016.

Those changes effectively compress the number of military personnel paid out of the base budget and accelerate the apparent savings from the planned reduction in end strength.

In its analysis of the FYDP, CBO estimated the personnel costs of the service members paid from the OCO budget and transferred those costs back to the base budget (see Table 2 on page 7).[8]

Box 2. Benefits Provided by the Department of Veterans Affairs

The Department of Veterans Affairs (VA) offers a variety of benefits to veterans of military service. The Veterans Health Administration (VHA) is responsible for health care.

Many other benefits—such as disability compensation (for veterans who incur service-connected disabilities); pensions (for wartime veterans with low income who are at least age 65 or, if younger, who are permanently and totally disabled because of nonservice injuries or medical conditions); life insurance; home loan subsidies; educational assistance; and educational and vocational counseling—are provided by the Veterans Benefits Administration (VBA). The National Cemetery Administration provides veterans with burial and memorial benefits.

VA's budget request for 2013 included $76 billion for the mandatory programs administered by VBA.[1] The remainder of VA's budget authority consisted of discretionary funding plus the authority to spend from the Medical Care Collection Fund (MCCF), which collects copayments from veterans for inpatient and outpatient care and for pharmaceuticals and collects third-party payments from veterans' insurance companies. VA requested $56 billion for medical programs and associated medical research and support, including $3 billion from the MCCF. Finally, adding $260 million for the National Cemetery Administration and $7 billion for department administration brings the entire 2013 budget request to $140 billion. (Neither the Department of Defense nor VA makes any accrual payments to account for future benefits that VA will provide to current service members when they separate or to current veterans as they age.)

Although eligibility criteria vary among VA's categories of benefits, all are contingent on the veteran's character of discharge. The military services determine whether a service member receives an honorable discharge, a general discharge under honorable conditions, a discharge under other than honorable conditions, or a bad conduct discharge. VA has developed a complex set of rules that implement the Code of Federal Regulations and determine whether a veteran's service record qualifies the veteran for particular VA benefits.[2] Veterans with honorable or general discharges are eligible for most VA benefits, although there are some exceptions. Veterans who are discharged under other-than-honorable conditions (but not bad conduct) are eligible for health care and related benefits for any disability incurred or aggravated in the line of duty during active service. Only veterans who receive an honorable discharge are eligible for educational assistance under the Post-9/11 GI-Bill.[3]

Eligibility for health care from VHA also depends on other considerations.

Generally, veterans of the active components of the military must have served 24 continuous months on active duty; reservists and National Guard members may be eligible if they are called to active duty under a federal order and they complete that service. Those broad criteria, however, do not necessarily guarantee access to medical treatment. VHA operates an enrollment system that assigns each beneficiary to one of eight categories to establish priority for using its health care services. Veterans with higher priority include those with service-connected disabilities, low income, or both. In January 2003, VHA imposed a general freeze (with some subsequent modifications) on new enrollments in the lowest priority group (Priority Group 8).[4]

The Veterans Programs Enhancement Act of 1998 (Public Law 105-368) guarantees access to VHA's health care system, after separation from active military service, to members of the armed forces who have served on active duty in combat operations since the law was enacted in November 1998; reservists and members of the National Guard who have served in combat operations are included under that guarantee. Specifically, the law gave combat veterans two years (starting from their date of separation from the military) to enroll and use VHA's health care system without requiring those veterans to document either that their income is below established thresholds or that they have service-connected disabilities—requirements that noncombat veterans must fulfill.

In 2008, lawmakers extended the enhanced eligibility period for care through VHA's health care system to five years.[5] Under those legislative authorities, VHA provides free health care for medical conditions directly or potentially related to a veteran's military service in combat operations for five years after separation. Veterans who had deployed to overseas contingency operations may continue to use VHA's services when the five-year period of enhanced eligibility ends, but their priority group for enrollment may change, depending on their disability status and income. In particular, such veterans may be moved to a lower priority group, including Priority Group 8, and incur the applicable copayments for health care services.

Eligibility for disability compensation (the most costly of the mandatory programs administered by VBA) is determined on the basis of character of discharge and the rating of disability assigned by VBA. (Veterans who claim disability compensation are exempt from minimum time-in-service requirements.)

To provide monthly disability benefits, VBA must have evidence that the veteran has a current disability, that the veteran incurred or aggravated an injury or disease while on active duty, and that the current disability is attributable to that serviceconnected medical problem. Once a veteran is judged to have met those criteria, VBA applies a rating of 0 percent to 100 percent disabling in 10 percentagepoint increments; that rating can be raised or lowered as a veteran's condition changes. Disability payments are determined by a veteran's disability rating: The greater the impairment, the larger the payment.

1. Spending for mandatory programs is determined through eligibility rules and other parameters in authorizing legislation rather than by appropriation of specific amounts each year. Funding for discretionary programs is provided in annual appropriation acts.
2. Department of Veterans Affairs, *M21-1MR, Compensation and Pension Manual Rewrite: Veterans Benefits Administration References,* Part 3, Subpart v, Chapter 1, Section B (updated March 7, 2006), http://go.usa.gov/yms.
3. Department of Veterans Affairs, "The Post-9/11 GI-Bill" (July 24, 2012), http://go.usa.gov/ym6.
4. Veterans in Priority Group 8 have no service-connected disabilities (or have service-connected disabilities that are ineligible for monetary compensation) and have annual income or net worth above VA's means-test threshold and regional income threshold. See Department of Veterans Affairs, "Health Benefits: Priority Groups Table" (August 20, 2012), http://go.usa.gov/YmfF.
5. See section 1707 of the National Defense Authorization Act for Fiscal Year 2008, Public Law 110-181, 122 Stat. 493.

Box 3. Projections of Defense Appropriations Under the Budget Control Act of 2011

The Budget Control Act of 2011 (BCA, Public Law 112-25) made several changes to federal programs, set caps on discretionary appropriations through 2021, and included automatic enforcement procedures that were to take effect if lawmakers failed to enact further legislation to reduce future budget deficits by specified amounts. At the time of the BCA's enactment, its caps on discretionary appropriations called for appropriations over the 2012–2021 period that would be roughly $0.8 trillion lower in nominal dollars during that period than if appropriations grew at the rate of inflation.

The BCA also stated that if legislation originating from a newly established Joint Select Committee on Deficit Reduction that was estimated to produce at least $1.2 trillion in deficit reductions (including an allowance for interest savings) was not enacted by January 15, 2012, automatic procedures for further limits on discretionary and mandatory spending would be triggered. Because no such legislation was enacted, those procedures are now scheduled to go into effect at the beginning of January 2013.

The triggering of the automatic enforcement procedures generated two changes to the way the caps will be implemented: It allocated the overall limits on discretionary appropriations between defense and nondefense budget functions by setting separate caps for each, and it reduced the total allowed funding below the original caps. For 2013, the additional reductions in allowed funding will be achieved by automatically canceling a portion of the budgetary resources already provided to that point (in an action known as sequestration); from 2014 to 2021, the reductions will be achieved by lowering the original caps on discretionary appropriations.[1] Under the BCA, there are no caps on funding for overseas contingency operations (OCO) or certain other activities.

Defense appropriations are defined as appropriations for budget function 050 (national defense), which includes the military activities of the Department of Defense (DoD), the nuclear weapons activities of the Department of Energy and the National Nuclear Security Administration, and the national security activities of several other agencies.[2] On average, during the past 10 years, funding for DoD has represented 95.5 percent of total funding for budget function 050.

Under the allocation of the BCA's caps on discretionary appropriations stemming from the automatic enforcement procedures— but before the reductions in the caps resulting from those procedures— total funding for national defense during the 2013–2021 period would be $290 billion less than what would have been provided if appropriations increased with inflation starting from the amount appropriated in 2012. The automatic reductions will lower the caps on discretionary funding for national defense by an additional $492 billion over the 2013–2021 period, with the reduction spread evenly at nearly $55 billion per year. The resulting caps start at $491 billion in 2013 and rise to $589 billion in 2021; the cap for 2021 is 15 percent lower than the amount appropriated for 2012, adjusted for inflation.

If DoD was assessed the same share of the $55 billion per year in automatic reductions for national defense as the department has received in funding historically, its budget authority would be reduced by about $52 billion each year.

For 2013, sequestration will apply both to the base budget and to funding for OCO, and the effect on the base budget alone is unclear; the amounts discussed here are estimated as though sequestration applied only to the base budget.

DoD's Funding Projected Under the Limits of the BCA
(Billions of dollars)

	Budget Control Act									
	Future Years Defense Program									
	2013	2014	2015	2016	2017	2018	2019	2020	2021	2022
	Nominal Dollars									
2013 FYDP and Extension[a]	526	534	546	556	567	607	620	641	661	680
Estimate of DoD's Funding Under the BCA Caps										
Before automatic reductions[b]	521	531	540	551	563	576	588	602	615	632 [c]
After automatic reductions[d]	469	479	488	499	511	524	536	549	563	578 [c]
	2013 Dollars									
2013 FYDP and Extension[a]	526	527	529	529	530	556	556	563	570	575
Estimate of DoD's Funding Under the BCA Caps										
Before automatic reductions[b]	521	524	524	525	526	527	527	529	530	534 [c]
After automatic reductions[d]	469	472	473	475	477	480	481	483	485	489 [c]

Source: Congressional Budget Office, Long-Term Implications of the 2013 Future Years Defense Program (July 2012), Table 1-4.

Note: DoD = Department of Defense; BCA = Budget Control Act of 2011; FYDP = Future Years Defense Program.

a. For 2013 to 2017, funding amounts correspond to DoD's 2013 FYDP. For the extension of the FYDP (2018 to 2022), CBO projects the costs of DoD's plans using the department's estimates of costs to the extent they are available and costs that are consistent with CBO's projections of price and compensation trends in the overall economy where the department's estimates are not available.

b. This estimate assumes that DoD would receive 95.5 percent of the funding limit for national defense before reductions arising from the BCA's automatic enforcement procedures, on the basis of DoD's average share of that funding in base budgets from 2002 to 2011.

c. CBO estimates this value as the value for 2021 plus an adjustment for expected inflation. Discretionary funding related to federal personnel is inflated using the employment cost index for wages and salaries; other discretionary funding is adjusted using the gross domestic product price index.

d. This estimate assumes that DoD would receive 95.5 percent of the funding limit for national defense after reductions arising from the BCA's automatic enforcement procedures, on the basis of DoD's average share of that funding in base budgets from 2002 to 2011.

DoD's base budget request for 2013 (net of OCO costs) exceeds estimated funding under the caps, before the automatic enforcement procedures are applied, by $5 billion (assuming DoD receives its historical share of funding for national defense). Through 2017, DoD's budgetary plan exceeds its estimated share of those caps by a total of $22 billion in nominal terms (compare the first and second rows of the table for the years 2013 through 2017). The annual gap widens to $46 billion by 2021 (the final year explicitly addressed by the BCA) because the Congressional Budget Office's extension of DoD's plan incorporates military and civilian pay raises that keep pace with the employment cost index, health care costs that track with national trends, and other sources of cost growth that are not accommodated by the caps. Assuming that the additional cuts that would result from the BCA's automatic enforcement procedures would be structured so that DoD continues to receive its historical share of funding for national defense, the cuts faced by DoD would be $52 billion per year—which would push funding far below the amounts in DoD's plans (see the third row of the table).

[1] For more information on those reductions, see Congressional Budget Office, *An Update to the Budget and Economic Outlook: Fiscal Years 2012 to 2022* (August 2012), Box 1-1.

[2] For information about the caps on discretionary budget authority for national defense, see Congressional Budget Office, *Final Sequestration Report for Fiscal Year 2012* (January 2012), Table 2.

Although DoD has proposed basic pay raises of 1.7 percent for 2013 and 2014—which are perhaps consistent with its projections of the employment cost index (ECI) for private-sector wages and salaries compiled by the Bureau of Labor Statistics—the department is planning to cap the pay raises at 0.5 percent in 2015, 1.0 percent in 2016, and 1.5 percent in 2017. Between the 5 percent cumulative reduction in end strength and the caps on pay raises, CBO projects that, on average, between 2013 and 2017, the MILPERS account will increase by 0.7 percent per year in nominal terms but decline by 1.0 percent per year in real terms.

Two Scenarios for Military Compensation

CBO has formulated a pair of scenarios that illustrate what could happen to the military personnel appropriation (and to the broader construct of military compensation) if all of the BCA's provisions—including sequestration (the automatic cancellation of a portion of budgetary resources) in 2013 and automatic reductions in the caps on funding for defense in 2014 through 2021—unfolded as written in current law. CBO developed an extension of DoD's 2013 FYDP using (to the extent they are available) the department's estimates of program costs or (where DoD estimates are not available) estimates that are consistent with the price and compensation trends that CBO projects for the overall economy. Full implementation of the BCA would require cuts relative to DoD's 2013 FYDP that average 10 percent per year over the department's five-year planning period; relative to the 2013 FYDP and its extension, the cuts would average 12 percent per year through 2022. This report does not include a corresponding analysis for a scenario in which the original BCA caps remain in place but sequestration and the subsequent automatic reductions are avoided. In such a case, the cuts would average less than 1 percent per year relative to the 2013 FYDP through 2017 and about 4 percent per year relative to the FYDP and its extension through 2022.

Under CBO's first scenario, cuts are made in equal proportion to DoD's RDT&E and procurement appropriations—the composite category that DoD calls *acquisition*—and all other appropriations remain as they are under the 2013 FYDP. To comply with the BCA, the RDT&E and procurement appropriations would be cut by 37 percent each over the 2013–2022 period relative to the 2013 FYDP and its extension. The procurement account, which stood at $105 billion in the base budget for 2012, would be cut by an average of about $50 billion a year (in nominal dollars) over the next decade. Under CBO's second scenario, across-the-board cuts are implemented that average

12 percent annually for all major appropriation accounts over the 2013–2022 period. Procurement funding between 2013 and 2022 would average about $80 billion (in nominal dollars) per year under the first scenario and about $110 billion under the second scenario.

Those scenarios are purely illustrative, and many other approaches and outcomes are plausible. For example, one could conceive of scenarios that disproportionately cut military compensation relative to the other portions of the defense budget, in turn requiring even larger reductions in end strength but preserving more funding for procurement. In the extreme, the same overall savings could be achieved if all other appropriation accounts remain as they are in the 2013 FYDP and its extension but military compensation is cut by an average of about 45 percent per year. All of the scenarios that would achieve the amount of savings that the BCA requires relative to the 2013 FYDP would have significant implications for the ability of the U.S. military to accomplish its missions.

Acquisition-Only Cuts

Under CBO's first scenario, all cuts mandated by the BCA would be made in equal proportion to the two acquisition appropriations: RDT&E and procurement. In contrast, the MILPERS and O&M appropriations (and therefore all elements of military compensation) would evolve according to DoD's FYDP for 2013. The procurement appropriation would be cut by an average of about $50 billion per year (in nominal dollars) or by 37 percent over the 2013–2022 period relative to the 2013 FYDP and its extension; the RDT&E appropriation would be cut by the same percentage, amounting to an average cut of about $25 billion per year (see Figure 1).

Although CBO has not developed a list of specific changes to DoD's procurement programs that could achieve those savings, it is clear that DoD would need to curtail or cancel many programs. For example, the Joint Strike Fighter (F-35) is DoD's largest procurement program. The three variants of the F-35 would replace, respectively, the Air Force's F-16s, the Navy's and Marine Corps' F/A-18s, and the Marine Corps' AV-8Bs. Because those aircraft are approaching the ends of their design lifetimes, DoD would almost surely purchase some other aircraft if procurement of F-35s was canceled.

CBO estimated last year that if DoD canceled the F-35 program and instead purchased additional F-16s for the Air Force and F/A-18s for the Navy and Marine Corps, the net savings in outlays through 2021 would be $48 billion. That sum would constitute 11 percent of the total by which the procurement appropriation would need to be cut relative to the 2013 FYDP under this scenario.[9] (Net savings would be $78 billion if the entire planned fleet of F-35s—not all of which would be purchased by 2021—was replaced with F-16s and F/A-18s.)

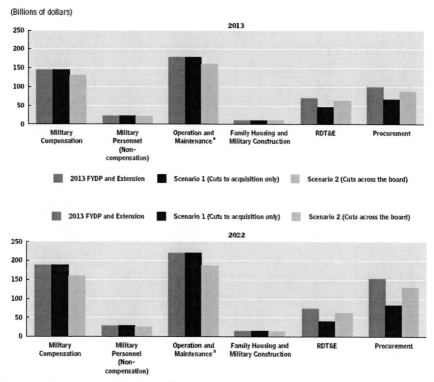

Source: Congressional Budget Office.

Notes: The 2013 FYDP and its extension are described in Congressional Budget Office, Long-Term Implications of the 2013 Future Years Defense Program (July 2012).

FYDP = Future Years Defense Program; RDT&E = research, development, test, and evaluation.

a. Excludes costs for the Defense Health Program because they are included in the category Military Compensation.

Figure 1. 2013 FYDP and Two Scenarios for the Defense Budget.

Across-the-Board Cuts

Under CBO's second scenario, all major appropriation accounts would be cut in equal proportion—by about 12 percent per year over the 2013–2022 period relative to the 2013 FYDP and its extension—to comply with the BCA (see Figure 1). The impact on the procurement appropriation is not nearly as dramatic as under the first scenario, declining in this instance by an average of $16 billion (in nominal dollars) relative to the FYDP and its extension over the next 10 years; RDT&E would fall by an average of $8 billion. Military compensation costs also would be cut by 12 percent. DoD has a range of options for achieving those savings: Trim end strength (beyond the declines already planned in the FYDP), reduce pay and benefits per service member, or pursue some combination of those two approaches.

Achieving those savings by reducing the number of service members would require more than a 12 percent reduction in end strength because such large reductions would take several years to complete and only a fraction of the eventual savings would be available during the transition years. For example, if the drop in end strength was phased in evenly over the next five years, a 17 percent cut in 2017 and later (relative to the 2017 value for end strength in the 2013 FYDP) would be needed to achieve savings that average 12 percent over the period through 2022. In all, that would mean shrinking the force by more than 240,000 people—more than currently serve in the Marine Corps (about 200,000). Achieving the same savings instead by reducing pay and benefits per service member gradually over a five-year period would require DoD to cut compensation by a similar percentage.

Achieving the same savings through a combination of reductions to end strength and reductions in pay and benefits would result in smaller cuts to each.

CURRENT CASH COMPENSATION

Current cash compensation for military personnel includes regular military compensation and numerous types of special pay and bonuses. Cash compensation changes over time according to formulas and in keeping with legislative action. Lawmakers authorized military pay raises for January 2008, 2009, and 2010 that each exceeded the percentage increase in the ECI for wages and salaries in private industry—a common benchmark — by 0.5 percentage points.[10] Beginning more than a decade ago, the housing allowance also has been restructured. In 2000, service members typically paid about 20 percent of their own housing costs, but by 2005, out-of-pocket expenses for the average military family had been eliminated. DoD reports that, as a result of those and other actions between January 2002 and January 2010, basic pay for the average service member increased by 42 percent (in nominal dollars), housing allowances increased by 83 percent, and the subsistence allowance increased by 40 percent.[11] CBO estimates that cash compensation increased by 52 percent overall during that period, whereas private-sector wages and salaries rose by 24 percent.

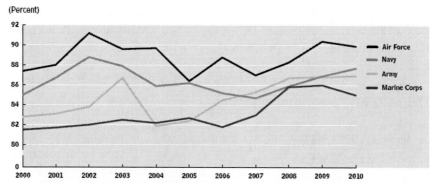

Source: Congressional Budget Office based on Department of Defense, Personnel and
        Readiness, Population Representation in the Military Services, Fiscal Year 2010
        (2011), Table D-32, http://go.usa.gov/ye8.
Note: Year-to-year continuation rates measure the proportion of personnel serving on
        active duty in the preceding year who are still in active-duty status during the year
        in question.

Figure 2. Year-to-Year Continuation Rates Among Active-Duty Enlisted Personnel.

Consistent with those increases in cash compensation, year-to-year continuation rates (the proportion of enlisted personnel serving on active duty in the preceding year who are still in an active-duty status during the year in question) were higher at the end of the last decade than they were at the beginning. The services saw declines in continuation rates of various degrees in the middle of the decade that were associated with lengthy deployments to Iraq and Afghanistan (see Figure 2). The Army partially mitigated its decline by using "stop-loss" policies to involuntarily extend soldiers' contracts.[12] The declines in continuation rates for all four services were reversed later in the decade when the U.S. economy worsened, deployments to Iraq tapered off, and increases in cash compensation continued to mount. Higher continuation rates help the military services to maintain or increase the number of people in the force and its readiness. In doing so, they increase the average tenure of the force, in turn boosting the compensation bill because the basic pay table rewards both pay grade and longevity.

Policies that limit annual raises could slow future growth in cash compensation. Those policies could take the form of capping increases in the basic pay table below the projected increase in the ECI, as DoD proposed in its 2013 budget submission.

Alternatively, DoD has the authority to set certain types of special pay, bonuses, and allowances within limits set in current law. DoD could reduce some of those rates of pay on its own initiative, or lawmakers could reduce those rates through legislative action.

Elements of Cash Compensation

DoD has used regular military compensation as a fundamental measure of military pay at least since 1962.[13] (RMC consists of basic pay plus subsistence and housing allowances and an estimate of the financial advantage that arises because those allowances are not subject to federal income taxes.)[14] All active-duty personnel (including guard and reserve personnel serving on active duty) are entitled to receive RMC.[15]

That compensation does not include most special pay, incentive pay, and other allowances that service members can receive. Special and incentive pay usually are awarded for obtaining particular skills or for performing hazardous duty, including deployment and combat. Members also can earn bonuses when they reenlist for several years, especially if they possess occupational skills that are in short supply.

DoD offers more than 60 types of special pay and bonuses, although an individual member might receive none or only a few at any time. For example, military personnel currently earn special pay at the rate of $225 per month (prorated daily for partial months) to serve in areas posing "imminent danger of being exposed to hostile fire or explosion of hostile mines."

In addition, service members may be paid up to $225 per month (not prorated, at DoD's discretion) if "exposed to hostile fire or a hostile mine explosion event" for even one day in a month.[16]

In its base budget request for 2013, DoD included $7 billion in special pay, incentive pay, and allowances (other than those for housing and food) for active-duty service members, amounting to about 6 percent of the department's proposed total payments to those members from the MILPERS appropriation.

Table 3. Procedures for Updating Military Compensation

	Basis for Update
Basic Pay	Percentage change in ECI (in accordance with the 2004 NDAA, unless overridden in the current session of Congress).[a]
Basic Allowance for Housing	Annual survey of rental prices for housing, including utility costs and renter's insurance, by size of residence and geographical area.
Pays and Allowances in Permanent Law (For example, family separation allowance, hazardous duty pay, and sea pay)	Payment amounts (rates and caps) set in law (Title 37, United States Code); subject to periodic legislative revision.
Bonuses and Special Pays Subject to Annual Reauthorization (For example, enlistment, reenlistment, and officer accession and retention bonuses)	Payment amounts (rates and caps) set in law (Title 37, United States Code). Lawmakers must reauthorize in each annual NDAA and may also periodically revise payment rates or caps.[b]

Source: Congressional Budget Office.

Notes: ECI = employment cost index for wages and salaries (the Bureau of Labor Statistics' index for the private sector); NDAA = National Defense Authorization Act.

a. The percentage change in the ECI is measured over the four quarters ending with the third quarter of the calendar year immediately preceding the budget submission (37 U.S.C. 1009, Adjustments of monthly basic pay). For example, the percentage change from the third quarter of 2009 to the third quarter of 2010 determined the pay raise for the 2012 budget submission; that budget was submitted in February 2011, and the pay raise took effect in January 2012.

b. The 2008 NDAA initiated a process under which lawmakers would set caps on broad groups of bonuses and forms of special pay, ceding to the Department of Defense the authority to set eligibility criteria and detailed pay levels consistent with those caps. Implementation of that authority is phased in over 10 years from the date of the NDAA's enactment and thus will be completed by January 28, 2018.

How Cash Compensation Has Evolved over Time

DoD can boost some elements of cash compensation within statutory limits, other elements are adjusted annually on the basis of the increase in a specified price index or other external metric, and still others require explicit legislative action (see Table 3).

The basic housing allowance is authorized through permanent law; DoD adjusts the amounts each year on the basis of local surveys of housing prices, without requiring either an explicit policy decision by the department or legislative action. Separately, lawmakers must explicitly act to renew various authorities that expire at the end of each year, such as those for bonuses to personnel trained in particular specialties. For example, the National Defense Authorization Act (NDAA) for Fiscal Year 2012 granted one-year extensions of authority to award certain bonuses and special pay to reserve forces, health care professionals, nuclear-qualified officers, and aviation officers.[17] That law also extended DoD's authority under title 37 of the United States Code to pay enlistment, reenlistment, and officer accession and retention bonuses; assignment incentive pay and special duty pay; and skill incentive pay and proficiency bonuses.[18] Other forms of pay and allowances, such as hazardous-duty pay and the family separation allowance, stay as they are currently until lawmakers adjust them.

The 2000 NDAA indexed annual increases in basic military pay through 2006 to the percentage increase in the ECI. In 2004, that temporary measure was overridden and a permanent link was established between the military pay raise and the percentage increase in the ECI.[19] As noted earlier, however, in enacting annual defense authorizations and appropriations, lawmakers often adjust the basic pay table by a percentage that deviates from the ECI, almost always in a direction that exceeds it (not since 1998 has the pay raise been smaller than the percentage increase in the ECI).

Various groups have advocated for such pay raises to rectify a perceived gap between basic military pay and the wages and salaries of comparable civilian workers. They generally begin with the presumption that the relatively large increases in military basic pay that were enacted in the early 1980s resulted in military pay scales that, by 1982, were largely comparable to those for equivalent work performed in the private sector.[20] They often go on to observe that the cumulative increase in basic pay since 1982 has fallen short of the cumulative increase in the ECI and draw the conclusion that military compensation is falling behind that for comparable civilian jobs.[21] In 1998 and 1999, the difference between the two cumulative increases—called the pay gap—peaked at 13.5 percent. The 11 military pay raises in excess of the ECI between January 2000 and January 2010, however, closed most of the gap, which stood at slightly more than 2 percent in 2010. That value was unchanged after the January 2011 and January 2012 pay raises, which just equaled the respective increases of 1.4 percent and 1.6 percent in the ECI for those years.

However, neither the concept nor the measurement of the pay gap is straightforward. First, the presumption that military and civilian pay were comparable or equivalent in 1982 is open to question. During Congressional testimony in advance of the 1982 pay raise, a department official in effect pushed the problem back 10 years by asserting that DoD's 1982 budget request would restore the comparability between military and civilian pay that existed in 1972.[22] However, the all-volunteer force had not been established by 1972; draft-era military pay, at least in the junior ranks, was set well below the pay scales that prevailed in civilian labor markets.[23] Therefore, the basis for measuring changes in relative pay starting from 1982 is tenuous.

Second, focusing on a single component of cash compensation—basic pay—gives an incomplete picture of the magnitude of the total cash portion of military compensation. Even assuming that pay comparability prevailed in 1982, the pay gap reversed its sign in 2002 when recomputed using the more comprehensive and appropriate measure of regular military compensation. By January 2010, the cumulative increase since 1982 in RMC had exceeded the cumulative increase in the ECI by 11 percent.[24]

Military and Civilian Compensation Compared

DoD has set a goal for the educational attainment of its enlisted personnel: At least 90 percent of those recruited to active duty in each service branch who have had no prior military service are to be high school graduates (a percentage that does not include recruits who hold the GED certificate), and at least 60 percent in each branch are to have scores above the national median on the Armed Forces Qualification Test, a screening instrument used by all branches of the military to assign enlisted personnel to specific military occupations. The services met all of the testing goals for the past decade, although the Army did so just barely in 2006, 2007, and 2008. The Army missed its goal for recruiting high school graduates in 2005 through 2008; in 2009, the Army rebounded, and 95 percent of its recruits were high school graduates (see Figure 3).

DoD has asserted that it does not expect to meet its goals for recruit quality unless RMC for enlisted personnel is set at the 70th percentile of earnings for civilians with some college education (many enlisted personnel go on to earn some postsecondary credits).[25] CBO's most recent detailed analysis, for calendar year 2006, showed that, on average, RMC exceeded the 75th percentile of earnings for comparably educated civilians, surpassing DoD's goal.[26] Thus, roughly three-quarters of civilians with comparable education had earnings that were lower than average RMC, and one-quarter had earnings that were higher. DoD recently updated that analysis, finding that average

RMC in 2009 had risen relative to the civilian wage distribution. The average RMC for enlisted personnel reached the 90th percentile relative to the combined comparison group consisting of civilians with high school diplomas, those with some college, and those with twoyear degrees; the average RMC for officers reached the 83rd percentile relative to the combined group of civilians with bachelor's degrees and those with a master's degree or higher.[27]

If the value of current noncash and deferred compensation (such as pensions and current and future benefits for health care) is included, total compensation for military personnel appears higher still than that for civilian workers in the economy. DoD has estimated that the value of current noncash and deferred compensation about equals that of RMC, effectively doubling the current cash pay of military personnel.[28] CBO's estimates are similar: For example, in 2006, noncash and deferred cash pay together boosted cash pay by about 80 percent for an unmarried sergeant (pay grade E-5 with six years of service) and by about 115 percent for a married sergeant.[29] By contrast, CBO has estimated that current noncash and deferred benefits (such as paid leave, health insurance, and retirement benefits) add an average of about 45 percent to the value of cash pay for civilians with a high school diploma or less and the same percentage for those with some college.[30]

Projected Costs of Cash Compensation

DoD's 2013 base budget included a request for a $135 billion MILPERS appropriation. The department plans to reduce active-duty end strength by a total of about 5 percent over the five years spanned by the 2013 FYDP, from 1,392,000 in 2013 to 1,320,000 by 2017.

However, DoD proposes that, in 2013, the personnel costs for 41,000 soldiers and 15,000 marines on active duty be shifted from the base budget to the OCO budget; the costs of the remaining 1,336,000 active-duty personnel in 2013 would be paid from the base budget. That procedure is followed, to a lesser degree, in the later years of the 2013 FYDP so that the steady-state force of 1,320,000 active-duty personnel is paid from the base budget starting essentially as early as 2014 and a diminishing number of personnel are paid from the OCO budget: 47,000 in 2014, 29,000 in 2015, and 12,000 in 2016. Incorporating DoD's plan for small increases in basic pay (discussed below), the 2013 FYDP projects MILPERS costs that are essentially flat at $135 billion (in 2013 dollars) over the period through 2017.

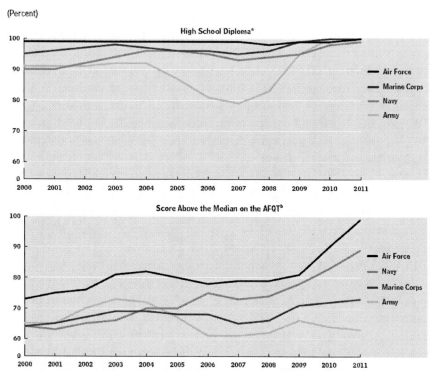

Sources: Congressional Budget Office based on Department of Defense, Personnel and
    Readiness, "Military Recruiting Results, Recruit Quality by Year Since FY 1973"
    (accessed November 8, 2012), http://go.usa.gov/V96; and James Hosek and
    others, Should the Increase in Military Pay Be Slowed? (RAND Corporation,
    2012), www.rand.org/pubs/technical_reports/TR1185.html.

Note: Accessions into the National Guard and the reserves are excluded.

a. The group with a high school diploma excludes recruits who hold alternative
    certification, such as the GED (General Educational Development) credential.

b. The Armed Forces Qualification Test (AFQT) is used to screen recruits to all
    branches of the military and to assign enlisted personnel to specific military
    occupations. Some high schools use the test to gauge students' interest in the
    military and other careers. The AFQT comprises arithmetic reasoning,
    mathematics knowledge, paragraph comprehension, and word knowledge.
    Percentile scores measure aptitude relative to the entire U.S. population between
    the ages of 18 and 23. Recruits who score above the national median are classified
    by the military into percentile categories relative to the U.S. population: I (93rd to
    99th percentile), II (65th to 92nd percentile), or IIIA (50th to 64th percentile)

Figure 3. Quality Trends Among Enlisted Recruits in the Active Military Who Did Not
Have Prior Military Service.

In its analysis of the 2013 FYDP, CBO estimated the personnel costs of the service members proposed to be paid from the OCO budget, and the agency shifted those costs back to the base budget.[31] As a result, CBO shifted about $5 billion in MILPERS costs back to the base budget in 2013, enlarging the MILPERS account from $135 billion to $140 billion in that year. With that procedure repeated for subsequent years, MILPERS costs would not be flat, CBO projects, but would decline from $140 billion in 2013 to $135 billion by 2017 (a real decline averaging 1 percent per year) as end strength falls throughout the five-year period.

Much of the historical increase in the cost per service member stems from increases in basic pay that have kept pace with or exceeded the growth rate of the ECI, which in turn grew more rapidly than the implicit price deflator for gross domestic product (GDP)—a common measure of overall inflation—in all but four years between 1981 and 2012. In contrast, DoD's plans for the 2013–2017 period do not include military pay raises that keep pace with the ECI. The department's plans include a 1.7 percent pay raise for 2014, which is below CBO's projection of the increase in the ECI for that year but is perhaps consistent with DoD's own projection of the ECI. For 2015 through 2017, DoD is proposing pay raises of 0.5 percent, 1.0 percent, and 1.5 percent, respectively—all deliberately smaller than the department's projection of ECI growth for those years. With that series of pay raises, basic pay would remain essentially flat in real terms (relative to the GDP deflator) over the FYDP period and lose a total of 11 percentage points of growth relative to CBO's projection of the ECI over those years. If, contrary to DoD's current plans, lawmakers restored pay raises at the ECI benchmark starting in 2014, CBO estimates that the MILPERS appropriation—instead of falling from $140 billion in 2013 to $135 billion (in 2013 dollars) by 2017—would increase to $145 billion by 2017, or by a total of almost 3 percent over the period.[32]

Controlling the Costs of Cash Compensation

Because basic pay is the largest element of cash compensation, policy alternatives that would limit annual raises hold considerable potential to slow growth in costs. Although retention of military personnel might suffer, that effect could be mitigated by boosting the amounts available for selective reenlistment bonuses (SRBs, which are offered to service members in hard-to-fill occupations). In the past, CBO has estimated budget options that would save roughly $6 billion in outlays over 5 years and $17 billion over 10 years by capping the annual increase in basic pay at 0.5 percentage points below the increase in the ECI for four years while increasing SRBs.[33] If a more stringent cap was applied or the same cap was maintained for a longer period, more could be saved.

One advantage of shifting some portion of cash compensation from basic pay to SRBs is that such bonuses are paid only to service members who have come to the end of an obligated term of service and are deciding whether to reenlist. That makes SRBs much more cost-effective than providing a pay raise to the entire force as a way to retain some fraction of the total. Furthermore, the services routinely award larger SRBs to people in military occupations in short supply; each branch is appropriated an annual SRB budget and is free to adjust allocations among the various occupations as conditions change during a given year. Finally, unlike pay raises, SRBs do not compound from one year to the next nor do they affect the value of retirement annuities.

MILITARY RETIREMENT BENEFITS

The military retirement system—predominantly a defined-benefit system that requires no contributions from employees—is a significant part of military compensation. The retirement system requires most military personnel to have 20 years of service for vesting, although disability retirement is sometimes granted sooner. As they approach retirement, service members can choose between one defined-benefit plan that offers a stated monthly payment and another that initially provides a lump-sum bonus during the member's 15th year of active service but then makes a smaller monthly payment once the member has retired. Active-duty retirees receive benefits immediately upon retirement, regardless of age—in some cases as early as age 37. Retirees from the reserves generally do not begin to collect benefits until they reach the age of 60. Since 2001, service members also have been eligible to participate in the federal Thrift Savings Plan, or TSP—a defined-contribution plan that is similar to a private-sector 401(k) plan—although generally without any matching contributions from the government.

To fund the retirement system, DoD sets aside an amount equal to a predefined percentage of basic pay in accrual payments while service members are on active duty. Future costs are dictated by the structure of the benefits, the mix of people receiving them, and inflation in the economy that determines the annual cost-of-living adjustment (COLA). For the future, costs could be managed by changing the vesting period, by changing the mix of defined benefits and defined contributions, or by some other means.

Alternative Retirement Plans

The defined-benefit portion of the military retirement benefit takes the form of an immediate annuity that is paid to military personnel who retire after at least 20 years. To protect against inflation, that annuity is boosted by a COLA equal either to the annual percentage change in the consumer price index for urban wage earners and clerical workers (CPI-W) or to that quantity minus 1 percentage point, depending on the retirement plan chosen by the service member.

High-3 Retirement Plan
For people who entered military service between September 8, 1980, and July 31, 1986, the annuity for a 20-year career has been set equal to 50 percent of the member's "High-3" basic pay, which is computed as the average of the 36 highest months of basic pay in the service member's career (the 50 percent factor is called the multiplier). The annuity increases with additional years of service, but until the end of 2006, the amount was capped at 75 percent of High-3 basic pay for members who retired after 30 or more years of service; that cap was subsequently lifted for people who retired after December 31, 2006.[34]

REDUX Retirement Plan
The Military Retirement Reform Act of 1986 (P.L. 99-348) created the REDUX retirement system for all personnel entering military service on or after August 1, 1986. The REDUX multiplier is 40 percent (rather than 50 percent) of a member's High-3 basic pay after 20 years of service, but it increases to 75 percent of basic pay after 30 years of service.

REDUX also provides only partial insulation from inflation rather than the full protection offered by the High-3 system. Until age 62, a retiree's annual COLA under REDUX equals the annual percentage increase in the CPI-W minus 1 percentage point. At age 62, the annuity payment is recomputed so that the retiree receives the same payment in that year under the REDUX system that would be paid under the more generous High-3 system: The multiplier is reset to the value it would have been under High-3 (for example, boosted from 40 percent to 50 percent for a 20-year career); the new multiplier is applied to the retiree's original highest 36 months of basic pay; and the current retirement annuity is recalculated by applying a full COLA (based on the cumulative growth of the CPI-W since the member's retirement, without the 1 percentage-point penalty). After the retiree passes age 62, the retirement annuity is again subject to a COLA equal to the increase in the CPI-W minus 1 percentage point (see Figure 4).

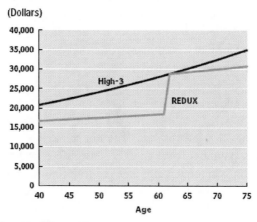

Source: Congressional Budget Office.

Note: Under the High-3 plan, monthly retirement pay after 20 years of service equals 50 percent of the average of the 36 highest months (three years) of basic pay in the service member's career; the 50 percent factor is called the multiplier. In the example shown, average pay for the highest three years of service is $41,550, and annual pay in the first year of retirement (at age 40) is half of that amount, or $20,775. Under the REDUX plan, the service member receives a Career Status Bonus, a lump-sum payment of $30,000 in the 15th year of military service, and the multiplier is 40 percent after 20 years of service. In the example, annual pay under the REDUX plan for the same service member in the first year of retirement is reduced to $16,620. Under High-3, retirement pay is adjusted annually on the basis of the consumer price index for all urban wage earners and clerical workers (CPI-W); under REDUX, retirement pay is adjusted annually by the CPI-W minus 1 percentage point, except for a one-time catch-up at age 62. Calculations were made under the assumption that the service member retired in 2011 at age 40 after 20 years of military service having served the final three years at pay grade E-6 (staff sergeant) and that the CPI-W increases at the rate of 1.5 percent per year starting in 2011.

Figure 4. Illustration of Military Retirement Pay, by Year of Age, Under High-3 and REDUX.

The first cohort of service members that would have been affected by REDUX began to retire in 2006. However, the 2000 NDAA preempted its implementation by giving military personnel a choice between two plans, both more generous than REDUX as initially conceived: the original High-3 plan or an enhanced REDUX plan.[35] Service members who anticipate retirement may choose during their 15th year of service either the High-3 plan or the less generous REDUX formula; those who choose the latter receive the Career Status Bonus, a lump-sum payment of $30,000, in the same year.[36] A service member who accepts that bonus but does not complete 5 more years to attain the full 20 years of military employment must repay a prorated share of the bonus as a penalty for separating early.

The rationale for setting the Career Status Bonus at $30,000 is not clear. That sum is not actuarially fair—it does not financially compensate the military retiree for what could easily be four decades of smaller annuity payments under the REDUX formula. The bonus has become smaller relative to forgone annuity payments over time because life expectancy has increased and because the bonus amount is not indexed to inflation and has been fixed at $30,000 since its inception. The bonus is taxable except when a service member's election of the REDUX option is finalized during a month in which the member is serving in a designated combat zone.[37] One report estimates that to achieve an actuarially fair outcome, the military retiree (unless serving in a combat zone) would need to have opportunities to invest the $30,000 bonus (net of applicable taxes for the year in which the bonus was received) at before-tax rates of return ranging from 10 percent to 20 percent (the exact rate would depend on the person's age, years of service, and pay grade at retirement). The same report also states that the number of marines choosing the REDUX option fell from 57 percent in 2001 to 15 percent in 2010, reflecting erosion in the inflation-adjusted value of the $30,000 bonus and, perhaps, a growing awareness among service members about the REDUX option's drawbacks.[38] (That report contains no data on the retirement choices made by soldiers, sailors, or airmen.)

Other Features of Military Retirement

Several other features of the military retirement system are noteworthy. The system offers a defined-contribution option, but DoD has decided not to exercise its authority to match service members' contributions. Active-duty personnel are generally vested in the defined-benefit component of their retirement plan after 20 years of service.

Those who retire after 20 years may begin to draw retirement pay immediately, but those who separate earlier do not receive any retirement benefits. That dichotomy has a major influence in shaping the military's force structure: It provides a strong incentive for midcareer personnel to remain in the military until they have completed 20 years of service but a much weaker incentive for those who have completed 20 years to continue their service into a third decade.

Thrift Savings Plan

An optional defined-contribution component for retirement saving, the TSP was made available to service members under the 2001 NDAA.[39] Military personnel may make tax-deferred contributions to TSP accounts that are equal to any percentage (1 to 100) of their basic pay, subject to annual dollar limits set by the Internal Revenue Code. Service members also may contribute up to the full amount of a Career Status Bonus or any reenlistment bonus received in a designated combat zone, subject to the combat-zone tax exclusion.[40]

During 2011, about 40 percent of active-duty service members participated in the TSP. (See Appendix A for a description of various other enhancements to the military retirement system enacted since 2000.)

The military services do not currently match service members' TSP contributions, as the federal government does for civilian employees, so the only cost to DoD is for administration. (The Army had a pilot program offering TSP matching contributions as an enlistment incentive from April 1, 2006, to December 31, 2008. The Army suspended the program in 2007 after analyzing its results.) Because TSP contributions are made from before-tax income, the program also reduces federal revenues.

Vesting

Members of the U.S. military are "cliff vested" in the retirement system. That is, they become eligible to receive benefits only upon reaching 20 years of service; there are no incremental vesting steps along the way. As a result, many people leave the service before attaining eligibility and so, apart from their own TSP accumulations, most service members earn no military retirement at all.

On the basis of the continuation rates that have been observed over the past few years, DoD currently estimates that 49 percent of active-duty officers and 17 percent of active-duty enlisted personnel will stay in the service long enough to earn nondisability retirement benefits.[41]

According to one estimate of the value to military personnel of those benefits, a service member would be willing to accept an immediate payment equal to 28 percent of the government's cost today of providing a dollar of retirement benefits in 10 years, even if he or she is certain to remain in the military until retirement.[42] The valuation of the retirement benefit would be smaller still for service members who are earlier in their careers and uncertain whether they will serve a full 20 years. However, the valuation steadily increases during the second decade of service, acting as an incentive to complete the full 20 years and qualify for retirement benefits. Evidence of the draw of retirement vesting (possibly along with other factors) is found in the annual continuation rates estimated from a cross section of enlisted personnel during 2010. Those rates exceeded 90 percent for people with at least 9 years of service, and they climbed to more than 97 percent for people with at least 15 years of service (see Figure 5). (The notches in Figure 5 at 4 years of service and again at 8 years reflect the proportion of people who choose not to reenlist at the end of the typical 4-year enlistment and reenlistment periods.) The continuation rate plummets to 63 percent during the 20th year because more than one-third of service members retire essentially as soon as they become eligible.

Accrual Funding

To account for its future liabilities in defined-benefit pensions for current service members, DoD makes accrual payments to the Military Retirement Fund for service members while they are still on active duty.[43] (See Appendix B for additional information regarding accrual accounting for the military retirement system.) The payments from the services' military personnel appropriations are assessed as a percentage of each member's basic pay, known as the normal cost percentage. DoD established normal cost percentages of 34.3 for active-duty personnel and 24.3 for reserve personnel in 2012.[44] Thus, for example, an active-duty E-4 (corporal) with between 48 months and 72 months of service will earn basic pay of $27,200 in 2012, for which DoD will make an accrual payment of $9,330 (0.343 × $27,200).

If a retiree chooses the enhanced REDUX option, the Career Status Bonus of $30,000 is paid immediately out of the military personnel appropriation for the fiscal year in which the service member makes his or her decision. If the service member instead chooses the High-3 option, both the multiplier and the COLA that determine the retirement annuity are higher than they would have been had REDUX been implemented as conceived in 1986; the eventual costs will be higher as well, so larger accrual payments are made. Using data from DoD's Office of the Actuary, CBO estimates that by 2017, the costs of the replacement for the REDUX system (the combined costs of the Career Status Bonus under the enhanced REDUX option and the larger accrual payments under the new High-3 option) will reach $2.3 billion (in 2013 dollars)— some 10 percent of the total retirement accrual and 1.6 percent of the projected MILPERS budget for that year.

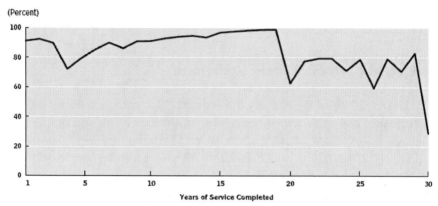

Source: Congressional Budget Office based on Department of Defense, Personnel and Readiness, Population Representation in the Military Services, Fiscal Year 2010 (2011), Table B-40, http://go.usa.gov/ye8.

Note: Continuation rates measure the proportion of personnel serving on active duty in the preceding year who are still in an active-duty status during the year in question.

Figure 5. Annual Continuation Rates Among Active-Duty Enlisted Personnel, 2010.

The choice of a flat normal cost percentage for all active personnel is essentially arbitrary. Moreover, it has been argued that the current accrual system leads to an ineffective allocation of resources because, for example, marines are less likely than members of the other services to reach retirement, yet the Marine Corps must apply the accrual rate used by the other services when it prepares its annual budget. On the basis of its analysis of data for a cross section of enlisted personnel during 2010, CBO estimates that only 40 percent of Marine Corps recruits will remain on active duty after the first four years of service, compared with more than 50 percent of Army recruits and more than 60 percent of recruits in the Navy and the Air Force. By using the same demographic data on the military population and the same projections of continuation rates used by the Office of the Actuary, it would be possible to design accrual schedules in which the accrual rate varies with the member's years of service. In particular, the accrual rates could be calibrated to reflect the fact that personnel with more seniority are more likely to remain in the military for the (fewer) additional years required to qualify for retirement. Decisions to increase the seniority mix of the force would then be tempered by the higher likelihood of incurring future retirement costs for those more senior personnel. However, such a system might be more cumbersome for the Office of the Actuary to maintain or for the military services to apply in their annual budgeting processes.

Projected Costs of Military Retirement

DoD's Office of the Actuary has estimated that outlays from the Military Retirement Fund to current beneficiaries will total $51.7 billion during 2012. Outlays are expected to increase to about $55 billion by 2017 and to $59 billion by 2022 (all in 2012 dollars).[45] Those estimates are based on a particular set of assumptions; even if the military's retirement policy remains stable, actual outlays could differ from projections to the extent that economic variables (such as interest rates) or demographic variables (such as life expectancy) deviate from their assumed values. Policy changes would have additional effects. For example, if the military services changed their policies in ways that increased the seniority mix of their forces, more service members probably would complete the 20 years necessary to earn nondisability retirement benefits. Or if a series of larger-than-planned pay raises was given, there also would be an increase in service members' High-3 basic pay, which determines annuity values for new retirees. Either policy change would lead to larger outlays from the Military Retirement Fund. Although the effects on outlays would occur gradually over the long term as increasing numbers of service members reach retirement under the new policies, DoD's Office of the Actuary would probably adjust the accrual rates in the short term.

Controlling the Costs of Military Retirement

Several proposals have been made for replacing the military's current system with a defined-benefit plan that partially vests at earlier points in a service member's career, or with a defined-contribution plan under which

DoD would match a service member's TSP contributions, or with a combination of those two plans. Those proposals could cost less or more than the current system, depending on how they were structured and implemented.

They also would affect the seniority mix of the armed forces, potentially damping the incentive for service members in their second decade of service to stay for a full 20 years.[46]

A potential drawback of a change from a defined-benefit system to (at least partially) a defined-contribution system is that the financial risk shifts to retirees, whose resources in retirement are no longer guaranteed by the federal government but instead depend on returns available in financial markets. Moreover, reductions in federal outlays that stem from retirement reform would be delayed for 20 years if all current service members were retained in the current system, as was the case with the introduction of REDUX. However, if the defined-benefit plan were made less generous on balance, then DoD's Office of the Actuary would probably reduce the accrual rates, and DoD would begin to see more immediate relief in the form of lower accrual payments to the Military Retirement Fund. DoD has not proposed any changes to its retirement system recently, but it has requested legislative language under which the Congress would establish a commission to review the retirement system and send recommendations to the President.[47]

THE MILITARY HEALTH CARE SYSTEM

Health care as provided under TRICARE is a noncash benefit for active-duty and retired service members; in fact, it is the most significant (and costly) deferred noncash benefit for retirees. Over the next decade, the cost per capita of providing TRICARE benefits is projected to increase at a rate substantially greater than inflation. Costs could be reduced by making changes in enrollment fees, deductibles, copayments, or other aspects of the benefits.

TRICARE

TRICARE health benefits are provided by a coordinated effort of the medical commands of the Army, Navy, and Air Force, under the supervision of the Assistant Secretary of Defense for Health Affairs. TRICARE offers various options, some of which are similar to employer-based health insurance plans:

- TRICARE Prime operates much like a health maintenance organization (HMO);
- TRICARE Extra is a preferred-provider network;
- TRICARE Standard is similar to a traditional fee-for-service plan;
- TRICARE Reserve Select is a premium-based health plan available to some members of the Selected Reserve and their families; and
- TRICARE for Life is a supplement for military retirees and their family members who also are eligible for Medicare.

Not all of those plans are available to all categories of beneficiaries, however. All 1.4 million active-duty military personnel are automatically enrolled in TRICARE Prime. In 2011, 2.0 million of the 2.4 million eligible family members of active-duty personnel (84 percent) were enrolled in Prime, as were 1.6 million of the 3.5 million retirees and family members who were not yet eligible for Medicare (45 percent). The roughly 2 million retirees and family members who are eligible for Medicare are not eligible to enroll in Prime or to use Extra or Standard, but they do qualify for the TRICARE for Life benefit.[48]

Active-Duty Personnel and Their Family Members

Active-duty military personnel receive all of their health care free of charge through TRICARE Prime, either at military medical treatment facilities (MTFs) or by referral from MTFs to civilian providers. CBO treats as compensation all of the costs for health care for activeduty personnel that are paid out of the base budget. CBO does not include in its tally any costs for medical care that are funded instead by the parallel budget for overseas contingency operations (see Box 4 on page 30).

Active-duty families may enroll in TRICARE Prime without paying an enrollment fee, and each enrollee is assigned a primary care manager—an individual provider or team of providers—either at an MTF or within the TRICARE network of civilian providers. All covered services are free to family members (with no deductibles or copayments other than for prescription drugs) as long as participants receive care either directly or by referral from the primary care manager. The civilian networks in the continental United States are managed under three regional contracts.[49]

Military Retirees and Their Family Members Who Are Not Yet Eligible for Medicare

Retired personnel who are not yet eligible for Medicare (generally people between the ages of 37 and 64) pay annual enrollment fees and copayments for most services. DoD has estimated that, in 2011, a typical military retiree and his or her family enrolled in TRICARE Prime paid $420 in copayments and other fees in addition to the $460 enrollment fee, for a total cost of $880. By contrast, DoD estimated that a civilian in the general U.S. population who enrolled in a family HMO plan offered by an employer would typically pay $4,010 in premiums (not including any share paid by the employer); with deductibles and copayments that average $980, that family would pay a total of $4,990 over the course of the year. Thus, the family enrolled in TRICARE Prime would have total out-ofpocket costs that are about 18 percent of what a similar family would pay in a civilian HMO (see Table 4).[50]

Table 4. Average Annual Out-of-Pocket Costs for Military Retiree Families Under TRICARE Plans and for Civilian Counterparts with Employment-Based Insurance, 2011, (Dollars)

	Premium or Enrollment Fee	Deductibles and Copayments	Total Annual Out-of-Pocket Costs
TRICARE Prime	460	420	880
Civilian HMO	4,010	980	4,990
TRICARE as a percentage of civilian plan	—	—	18
TRICARE Standard or Extra	0	1,000	1,000
Civilian PPO	4,020	1,360	5,380
TRICARE as a percentage of civilian plan	—	—	19

A corollary of the lower deductibles and copayments (totaling $420 versus $980) is that TRICARE Prime enrollees use that system significantly more than comparable civilian beneficiaries use their health care systems. Including not only the retiree families described in this section but also active-duty families (who pay essentially no out-of-pocket costs), DoD estimates that the rates of use for inpatient, outpatient, and pharmacy services are much higher among Prime enrollees than among enrollees in civilian HMOs.[51] DoD's information is consistent with the results of studies of civilian health insurance showing that copayments, deductibles, and the restrictions of managed care can significantly decrease spending on health care. Those studies also show that, up to a point, increased cost sharing may reduce unnecessary use of health care without adversely affecting beneficiaries' overall health.[52]

Box 4. Incremental Health Care Costs Related to Combat

Some medical care currently provided by the Department of Defense (DoD) consists of treatment for combat injuries and other conditions associated with deployment, and some of that care is funded not in DoD's base budget but rather in its budget for overseas contingency operations.

Although the Congressional Budget Office (CBO) does not include the incremental costs for wartime medical care in the agency's definition of military compensation, at least some of those costs represent noncash compensation that is conceptually equivalent to cash pay for hazardous duty, which is included in the definition. (The analysis in this study includes only the health care provided by DoD while service members are on active duty; it excludes the care provided by the Department of Veterans Affairs to members who have left the service.)

It is difficult to comprehensively estimate the amount that DoD spends on wartime medical care. Some of that care—provided at mobile field hospitals and aboard hospital ships, for example—is under the jurisdiction of the Army, Navy, and Air Force medical commands rather than the centralized Defense Health Program, and it is not readily identifiable in the budget documents of the various service branches.

Incremental care under the jurisdiction of the Defense Health Program has several other elements:

- Transport of service members from Landstuhl Regional Medical Center in Germany (the staging area for evacuation from Iraq or Afghanistan) to the United States,
- Treatment of combat injuries at military treatment facilities in the United States,
- Hiring of civilian and contractor personnel at U.S. treatment facilities to cover for military personnel who are deployed,
- Administration of pre- and postdeployment medical examinations, and

- Provision of medical and dental care to members of the reserves and the National Guard who are mobilized for wartime deployment and who otherwise would not be eligible to receive free care.

The Defense Health Program budget request for 2013 included $1.0 billion for operation and maintenance costs associated with combat operations.[1] CBO does not include those costs in its tally of military compensation, which is restricted to costs paid out of the base budget.

1. Department of Defense, Defense Health Program, Fiscal Year (FY) 2013 Budget Estimates—Operation and Maintenance, Procurement, Research, Development, Test and Evaluation, vol. 1, Justification of Estimates (February 2012), pp. 132–135, http://go.usa.gov/p5q.

Military retirees are increasingly relying on TRICARE as the primary source of health care coverage for their families. The migration of retirees from private health insurance to TRICARE is one contributor to the rapid increase in TRICARE spending in the past decade. The family enrollment fee for TRICARE Prime, while remaining fixed at a nominal value of $460 per year, declined in real terms (accounting for inflation) by 21 percent between 2001 and 2011. (As of October 1, 2011, annual enrollment fees for new enrollees were boosted to $260 for singles and $520 for families; the enrollment fees for all enrollees will be set at those amounts plus an inflation adjustment starting October 1, 2012. See Appendix C for the legislative history of the TRICARE benefit.) At the same time, the average employee's share of the family premium for an employment-based insurance plan in the private sector increased by 80 percent in real terms.[53] Concurrent with those developments, the proportion of military retirees with private health insurance dropped by half, from about 50 percent to 25 percent, and the proportion enrolled in TRICARE Prime increased from about 30 percent to 50 percent. (The remaining one-quarter of retirees had neither private health insurance nor were enrolled in TRICARE Prime, although many relied on TRICARE Standard or Extra or had access to other federal programs.) DoD estimates that about 730,000 more retirees and family members under age 65—some 45 percent of the 1.6 million enrollees in that category—now rely primarily on TRICARE Prime (and not private health insurance) than would be the case if the relative premiums and out-of-pocket costs in the two sectors remained as they were in 2001.

Military retirees under the age of 65 who do not choose to enroll in TRICARE Prime may receive benefits under TRICARE Extra or Standard without paying an enrollment fee, and they are eligible for space-available care at MTFs. Participants in TRICARE Extra or Standard must pay an annual outpatient deductible of $150 (for single coverage) or $300 (for family coverage). During 2011, a typical family in those plans paid about $1,000 in TRICARE deductibles and copayments, whereas a civilian family in an employment-based preferred-provider plan would typically pay $4,020 in premiums (not including the share paid by the employer) and, including deductibles and copayments that average $1,360, a total of $5,380 over the course of the year. Thus, the family that relies on TRICARE Extra or Standard would pay total out-of-pocket costs that are about 19 percent of what a civilian family would pay in a preferred-provider plan (see Table 4).[54]

DoD pays for health care provided to non-Medicareeligible retirees and their family members contemporaneously; the department does not make accrual payments to fund future costs for that beneficiary group.

Military Retirees and Their Family Members Who Are Eligible for Medicare

In 2002, DoD introduced a new benefit, TRICARE for Life, to supplement Medicare for military retirees and their family members who also are eligible for Medicare (a group known as dual-eligibles).[55] Before TFL was created, retirees and their families would lose access to the civilian portion of their TRICARE benefits once they became eligible for Medicare, although they retained their eligibility for in-house care at MTFs (so long as there was space available) and access to free prescription drugs dispensed by MTF pharmacies. Several military retirees filed lawsuits against the federal government, claiming variously that they had been promised low-cost or free health care for the remainder of their lives; that they were entitled to receive that care at military treatment facilities; and that if such care was not available at MTFs, the federal government was obliged to purchase that care on their behalf from the private sector. The courts consistently ruled that, although military recruiters may have enticed recruits with promises of free lifetime medical care, those promises did not bind the military to provide such care; only the Congress and the President could establish permanent health care benefits. (See Appendix D for a discussion of whether DoD was legally bound to provide military personnel with lowcost health care in retirement.) Lawmakers then acted to establish TFL. With the introduction of TFL, TRICARE became the second payer to Medicare for those beneficiaries. Dualeligibles now must enroll and pay the monthly Medicare Part B premium to remain eligible for TRICARE. (Medicare Part B covers doctors' services, outpatient care, home health services, and other medical services including some preventive services.) Having done so, when people in that group receive medical services that are covered by both Medicare and TRICARE, Medicare pays the portion of the service's cost allowed under its rules, and TRICARE pays most, if not all, of the Medicare deductibles and coinsurance. When dual-eligibles receive medical services that are covered by TRICARE but excluded by Medicare, TRICARE covers most of the costs, although beneficiaries may still be responsible for some cost sharing. As of April 1, 2001, beneficiaries who are at least age 65 are eligible for the full TRICARE pharmacy benefit if they also are enrolled in Medicare Part B; otherwise, their drug benefits are limited to the prescriptions available at MTF pharmacies. Medicare-eligible beneficiaries also can enroll in prescription drug plans under Medicare Part D, but they need not enroll in such a plan to exercise their TRICARE pharmacy benefits. No copayments are assessed for formulary drugs (generic and brand-name drugs that DoD encourages its clinicians to prescribe and that it provides to beneficiaries free or at a reduced outof-pocket cost) dispensed at MTF pharmacies or for formulary generic drugs obtained by mail order; other types of drugs (including all drugs obtained from retail pharmacies) entail modest copayments.[56]

During fiscal years 2000 and 2001—just before the introduction of TFL— 88 percent of Medicare-eligible military retirees purchased Medicare supplemental insurance (in addition to Medicare Part B) or were covered by Medicaid. By "wrapping around" the Medicare benefit, TFL would seem to make it unnecessary for those families to continue to pay for Medicare supplemental insurance. Although purchases of supplemental insurance have fallen precipitously, DoD reports that as recently as 2011, almost 20 percent of dual-eligible families still purchased either a Medicare supplement (apart from TFL) or used some other alternative to the combination of Medicare and TFL. Those families continued to purchase such policies perhaps because they were unaware of or lacked confidence in the TFL benefit or because they wanted to have overlapping coverage.[57] Another possible explanation is that some participants might be Medicare-eligible military retirees who are still employed in the civilian sector and choose to retain employment-based family coverage in order to continue coverage for a spouse who is not yet eligible for Medicare; dropping an employmentbased plan in favor of a combination of

Medicare and TFL could leave those spouses without any ready source of medical insurance.

Table 5. DoD's Funding Request for the Defense Health Program, 2013

	Billions of Dollars
Military Personnel	
Pay and allowances of medical personnel	8.2
Accrual payments into the MERHCF	6.7
Subtotal	14.9
Operation and Maintenance	
Direct care at military medical treatment facilities and administrative costs	14.1
Purchased care and contracts	14.2
Pharmaceuticals	3.8
Subtotal	32.0
Military personnel and operation and maintenance	46.9
Procurement	0.5
Research, Development, Test, and Evaluation	0.7
Total, Defense Health Program	48.1

Source: Congressional Budget Office.

Notes: All entries are for the base budget only and exclude additional funding requested for overseas contingency operations.

DoD = Department of Defense; MERHCF = Medicare-Eligible Retiree Health Care Fund.

Military Reserve Personnel

Members of the reserves and National Guard become eligible for TRICARE and receive the same benefits as active-duty service members when they are activated (called or ordered to active duty for more than 30 consecutive days). They also may qualify for up to 180 days of a "preactivation benefit" if they receive advance orders to report to active duty at a future date.

Some members of the Selected Reserve may enroll in the TRICARE Reserve Select program. DoD sets the premium equal to 28 percent of the actuarial cost of coverage, and it updates that premium annually on the basis of the program's costs during the preceding calendar year.

Members of the Retired Reserve who are qualified for a nonregular (deferred) retirement but have not reached age 60 are eligible for the TRICARE Retired Reserve program, but they must pay 100 percent of the actuarial cost of their coverage; there is no government subsidy.

Projected Costs of the Military Health Care System

The largest element in DoD's $48 billion request for the Defense Health Program in 2013 is $32 billion in O&M funding: $14.1 billion for direct care provided in MTFs and other administrative activities, $14.2 billion for purchased care and contracts, and $3.8 billion for pharmaceuticals (see Table 5). Although they are not shown separately, the costs of pay and benefits for the 60,000 full-time-equivalent civilian employees who are assigned to the military health care system to provide health care and administrative services are included in the O&M total in Table 5. In addition, DoD plans to assign some 86,000 military personnel to the military health care system; the cost of their pay and benefits—$8.2 billion—would be collectively borne by the MILPERS accounts of the Army, Navy, and Air Force.[58] DoD also requested funding for health care of less than $1 billion each for the procurement and RDT&E appropriations.

Finally, in 2013, DoD plans to contribute $6.7 billion from the MILPERS accounts into the Medicare-Eligible Retiree Health Care Fund to account for the future health care of current service members. DoD projects that the cost for the department to provide health care to Medicare-eligible retirees and their families will exceed the accrual contribution. Specifically, DoD anticipates outlays of $9.7 billion from the MERHCF in 2013 to reimburse TRICARE providers and MTFs for care delivered to that group of beneficiaries.

DoD has set annual accrual rates for the MERHCF of about $4,400 for active-component personnel and $2,400 for reserve-component personnel for 2013. Those rates are roughly $1,000 less than prevailing rates in 2012 because of two recent policy changes and one adjustment to the economic assumptions of DoD's Office of the Actuary. Specifically, DoD achieved full implementation of a program to collect rebates from drug manufacturers at retail pharmacies, and it implemented section 708 of the 2012 NDAA, which places certain limitations on enrollment of military retirees in the Uniformed Services Family Health Plan.[59] Also, during 2011, the Office of the Actuary lowered its estimate of the nominal growth rate in per capita medical spending for dual-eligibles, from 6.25 percent to 5.75 percent per year.

As part of its budget request for 2007, DoD made a set of proposals that it labeled "Sustain the Benefit" that increased the amount beneficiaries would pay out of pocket for medical care; the department subsequently submitted amended versions of that plan in its 2008 and 2009 budget requests. The 2009 proposal would have substantially increased the annual enrollment fee for

TRICARE Prime for military retiree families who were not yet eligible for Medicare, increased various copayments under TRICARE Prime, instituted an annual enrollment fee for TRICARE Extra or Standard, and increased the annual family deductible under TRICARE Extra or Standard. All of the Sustain the Benefit proposals were blocked by Congressional action (see Appendix C for more details).

DoD's budget requests for 2010 and 2011 did not call for higher TRICARE fees, but the 2012 request led to an increase—from $460 to $520 per year—in the family enrollment fee for TRICARE Prime. DoD's budget request for 2013 reprises several aspects of its earlier Sustain the Benefit proposals:

- Institute an annual fee for Medicare-eligible military retirees who enroll themselves or their families in TFL;
- Increase the annual fee that military retirees who are not yet eligible for Medicare pay to enroll themselves or their families in TRICARE Prime;
- Institute an annual fee for non-Medicare-eligible military retirees to enroll themselves or their families in TRICARE Standard or Extra;
- Increase the annual deductibles for non-Medicareeligible military retirees who enroll themselves or their families in TRICARE Standard or Extra; and
- Adjust the pharmacy copayments for active-duty family members and for retirees and their families as an incentive to purchase mail-order and generic drugs.[60]

DoD estimated that, over the period from 2013 through 2017, those initiatives could save $5.5 billion in the department's O&M appropriation and $7.4 billion in accrual payments into the MERHCF. The House of Representatives' version of the 2013 NDAA rejects DoD's proposal.[61] The full Senate has not yet voted on its version of that NDAA.

CBO has projected DoD's health care costs through 2022. CBO based its projections of costs in part on average growth rates within the military health care system between 2006 and 2011, which, in most categories, have been significantly higher than the corresponding rates in the national economy. For example, DoD's spending per user for purchased care and for direct care at MTFs increased at real rates of 4.2 percent and 3.2 percent per year, respectively, compared with a national average of 1.3 percent per year for a comparable composite category of hospital care and physician and clinical services in the broader economy.[62] However, CBO does not view the faster growth rates within military health care as likely to continue unabated. Instead, CBO expects DoD's costs to decelerate, eventually reaching a growth rate in 2030 (a year that is beyond the horizon of the current analysis) of around 1 percentage point above the growth of per capita GDP, an assumption that is roughly consistent with estimates in CBO's *The 2012 Long-Term Budget Outlook.*[63]

(Billions of 2013 dollars)

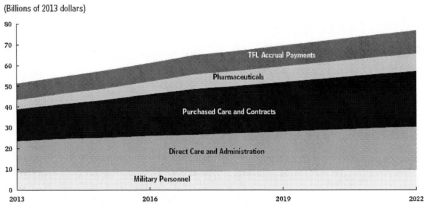

Source: Congressional Budget Office, Long-Term Implications of the 2013 Future Years Defense Program (July 2012).

Note: TFL = TRICARE for Life.

Figure 6. Projected Costs of the Military Health System.

DoD requested $48 billion for the military health system in 2013, but lawmakers have a long history of denying the department's requests to increase out-of-pocket costs paid by TRICARE beneficiaries. Therefore, CBO used the assumption that DoD's proposed fee increases would not take effect and thus would produce no savings, and the agency's projection is for health care costs of $51 billion in 2013. CBO projects that health care costs will ris to $65 billion (in 2013 dollars) by 2017, reflecting an average real growth rate of 6.0 percent per year over the next five years (see Figure 6). (In contrast, DoD projected that the average real growth rate would be about 2.6 percent during the same period.) The 6.0 percent real growth rate embodies several effects beyond the growth rates in annual spending per user for certain medical services delineated above. CBO projects that spending on other categories of care, such as pharmaceuticals, will increase more rapidly than spending on patient care.

Also, because the enrollment fees and copayments under TRICARE remain below the amounts that many military retirees would pay under their employment-based insurance plans, CBO projects that the number of retirees who will choose to enroll in TRICARE Prime will continue to increase (albeit slowly) for several years into the future, adding still more to the total costs for that group.

CBO projects that the faster cost growth within DoD will taper off in the second half of the next decade, averaging 3.4 percent per year between 2017 and 2022. That rate implies an overall average rate of growth between 2013 and 2022 of 4.6 percent per year, in turn implying that military health care costs will reach $77 billion by 2022.

Controlling the Costs of Military Health Care

Several proposals have been made for controlling the costs of military health care by raising enrollment fees, deductibles, or copayments. Depending on the details, those proposals could save DoD as much as $10 billion per year.

Higher enrollment fees mean larger collections by the government, and they also could encourage some retiree families to turn to employment-based health plans, which would save money for the government. Higher deductibles and copayments could lower the government's costs both by encouraging participation in employment-based plans and by trimming the use of medical services among the remaining TRICARE participants.

CBO estimated that the 2009 Sustain the Benefit proposal, if enacted, would have reduced DoD's spending by $5 billion in 2011, the third year covered by the proposal and the first year in which all fees would have reached their new (higher) amounts.[64]

In the past, CBO has estimated that DoD could reduce its spending on military health care by increasing the out-of-pocket costs paid by military retirees who are not yet eligible for Medicare (saving $10 billion in outlays over 5 years and $28 billion over 10 years) or by precluding that same group from enrolling in TRICARE Prime altogether, allowing them instead to pay to enroll in TRICARE Standard or Extra (saving $37 billion in outlays over 5 years and $105 billion over 10 years).[65]

APPENDIX A: ENHANCEMENTS TO THE MILITARY RETIREMENT SYSTEM ENACTED SINCE 2000

The National Defense Authorization Act for Fiscal Year 2000 (NDAA, Public Law 106-65) gave military personnel a choice between the "High-3" retirement plan and an enhanced REDUX retirement plan. Military personnel who chose the latter plan could retire after 20 years of service at 40 percent of their basic pay and receive partial insulation from inflation (the High-3 plan offered a 50 percent annuity and full inflation protection); they also would receive a $30,000 lump-sum payment during their 15th year of service.[1] Four other components of military retirement have changed as a result of legislation enacted since 2000:

- The Social Security offset for the Survivor Benefit Plan has been eliminated,
- Certain reservists are now eligible to receive retirement pay before reaching the age of 60—the age to which that pay had previously been deferred,
- The rules regarding concurrent receipt of disability and retirement benefits have been changed, and
- The cap on the multiplier for regular military retirement pay has been raised.

Survivor Benefit Plan

Military retirees can elect to pay a premium that will allow their surviving spouses to continue to receive a portion of their retirement pay. In the past, once the surviving spouse reached the age of 62 and became eligible for Social Security benefits, payments under the Survivor Benefit Plan were cut from 55 percent to 35 percent of the retirement pay that the service member would have received.

However, the 2005 NDAA (P.L. 108-375, section 644) phased out the reduction in payments below 55 percent of retirement pay; implementation was spread over five increments beginning on October 1, 2005, and ending on April 1, 2008.[2]

Early Receipt of Retirement Pay by Certain Reservists

The 2008 NDAA (P.L. 110-181, section 647) changed the ages at which some reservists who have served in Iraq, Afghanistan, and elsewhere become eligible to receive retirement pay.[3] Regular active-duty military personnel qualify for full retirement benefits after 20 years of service, regardless of age. By contrast, most reservists with 20 years of qualifying service must wait until reaching the age of 60 to receive retirement pay and health care benefits.

The 2008 NDAA created a new formula to allow some retired reservists to receive retirement pay before reaching age 60. Specifically, for every 90 days within a fiscal year that a reservist is on active duty or performs active service, the traditional eligibility age is reduced by three months. Although the period of service need not be continuous, credit is given only in 90-day increments. So a reservist who serves a six-month tour (180 days) may draw retirement pay at age 591/2 instead of waiting until age 60 (and if the tour lasts 200 days, the reservist would still draw retirement pay at 591/2).

The provision applies only to reservists who are activated under the statutory authorities specified in the 2008 NDAA and to service that occurred after the law's enactment on January 28, 2008. No reservist may receive retirement payments before age 50; the earliest age of eligibility for medical benefits remains at 60.

Concurrent Receipt

Through calendar year 2003, military retirement pay was reduced dollar for dollar by the amount of disability compensation a retiree received from the Department of Veterans Affairs. (Many eligible retirees still chose to receive disability compensation because those benefits are not subject to federal income taxes.) As a result of successive pieces of legislation, starting with the 2003 NDAA (P.L. 107-314), several classes of retired military personnel now can receive military retirement pay without any offset for compensation for service-connected disabilities. For example, under a program that will be fully phased in by January 2014, retirees with 20 or more years of service who are rated at least 50 percent disabled will face no offset between the two benefits.[4] The 2004 NDAA (P.L. 108-136) further requires that the U.S. Treasury, rather than the Department of Defense, make the accrual payments to fund concurrent receipt.[5] The Treasury made accrual payments of $4.8 billion in

2011, an amount projected by the Office of the Actuary in the Department of Defense to grow to $5.6 billion (in 2012 dollars) by 2017.[6]

The Cap on the Multiplier for Regular Retirement

The 2007 NDAA (P.L. 109-364) lifted the cap on the multiplier, which had been set at 75 percent of basic pay, that is used to set the annuity amount for nondisability retirement from the active military.[7] The multiplier for most active military personnel who retired after December 31, 2006, was reset at 2.5 percent times the years of service credited—without the cap—so that very senior personnel (those with more than 30 years of service) could retire at more than 75 percent, and conceivably at more than 100 percent, of the average of their highest 36 months of basic pay (the High-3). Also, section 601 of the same law modified the basic pay table to include longevity increases for continued service into the fourth decade for very senior enlisted personnel (E-9, the highest pay grade), warrant officers (W-5, the highest rank), and commissioned officers (O-8 through O-10, or two-star through four-star generals and admirals). Those longevity increases were perpetuated in subsequent across-the-board increases to the basic pay table.

APPENDIX B: ACCRUAL ACCOUNTING FOR THE MILITARY RETIREMENT SYSTEM

Accrual accounting is a method of accounting in which revenues are recognized in the period earned and costs are recognized in the period incurred, regardless of when payment is received or made.[1] Proponents assert that accrual accounting leads to better-informed decisionmaking because the full costs of a policy become apparent during the year in which that policy is adopted. If an increase in the number of military personnel is under consideration, for example, the full costs— including the future retirement costs of those additional personnel—become part of the decision calculus.

On October 1, 1984, the Department of Defense (DoD) adopted accrual accounting for the military retirement system. The Military Retirement Fund was established "in order to finance on an actuarially sound basis liabilities of the Department of Defense under military retirement and survivor benefit programs."[2] The flows of money into the fund come from several sources:

- Amounts paid into the fund by DoD or by the U.S. Treasury;
- Any amount appropriated to the fund; and
- Any return on the assets of the fund, which are invested in U.S. Treasury securities.

Payments out of the fund are made to military retirees and their survivors. Although participants in the other uniformed services—including members of the Coast Guard, officers of the Public Health Service, and officers of the National Oceanic and Atmospheric Administration—are covered under retirement systems that are similar to that of DoD, those systems are separate from the Military Retirement Fund.

Not all payments into the fund are made by DoD. The National Defense Authorization Act for Fiscal Year 2004 requires that the Treasury, rather than DoD, make the accrual payments to fund concurrent receipt—the ability of several classes of retired military personnel to receive military retirement pay without any offset for payments they receive from the Department of Veterans Affairs in compensation for service-connected disabilities.[3] Thus, under a program that will be fully phased in by January 2014, retirees with 20 or more years of service who are rated at least 50 percent disabled will face no offset between the two benefits.

The balance in the Military Retirement Fund is held in special-issue (nonmarketable) Treasury securities. The Secretary of the Treasury determines the interest rates for those securities, taking into consideration current yields for marketable Treasury securities of comparable maturity. The balance in the fund is an asset for the military retirement system but a liability for the rest of the federal government. As such, it is a measure of the amount that the government has the legal authority to spend on military retirement payments under current law, although it has little relevance in an economic or budgetary sense. Payments from the fund to beneficiaries count as federal spending; the accrual contributions and the amortization payments from the Treasury are intergovernmental transactions that have no net effect on federal outlays.

When accrual accounting began, no funds had been set aside for service members who had already retired, and many who were serving at the time remained in the military long enough to retire. Starting in 1985, DoD made accrual payments on behalf of that latter group, but the payments started too late to fully fund the group's retirement benefits (including survivors' benefits). The Treasury makes accrual payments to fund the remaining liability for that group plus the liability for service members who had already retired by 1985. DoD estimated the initial unfunded liability at $529 billion (in 1984 dollars) as of September 30, 1984.[4] That balance could have been amortized in several ways. DoD's Board of Actuaries at first determined that it could amortize the unfunded liability by making 60 annual payments, each equal to 33 percent of the total DoD had spent on basic pay in 1983. On several subsequent occasions, in light of legislative changes to retirement benefits and changes in economic assumptions, the board revised the payment amounts and the period over which the unfunded liability would be amortized.[5] As of September 30, 2010, the unfunded liability stood at $904 billion (in 2010 dollars).

However, the payment schedule is fundamentally arbitrary, so flows into the fund do not provide a useful measure of how much military retirement is costing the federal government in a given year. DoD's Office of the Actuary reports that outlays from the Military Retirement Fund totaled $50.8 billion during 2011. On the other side of the ledger, flows into the fund consisted of $19.8 billion from DoD, $4.8 billion from the Treasury to cover payments to military retirees under concurrent receipt, $61.4 billion from the Treasury toward amortizing the unfunded liability, and investment income of $21.4 billion (in all, $107.4 billion).[6] The size of the Treasury's amortization payment—the largest single flow into the fund and more than half of the total—is an artifact of the current plan to fully amortize the unfunded liability by 2025. A faster amortization schedule would require a larger annual contribution from the Treasury, and a slower schedule would require a smaller annual contribution.

The distinction between outlays from the Military Retirement Fund and flows into the fund is not always clear in policy discussions of the military retirement system.

For example, the Defense Business Board—an internal advisory panel within DoD—has issued a study on the military retirement system that proposes use of the total inflow of $107.4 billion as a metric for comparing the current defined-benefit system with an alternative defined-contribution system.[7]

Yet the emphasis on flows into the fund rather than outlays from the fund turns attention away from federal spending. Furthermore, the Treasury's amortization payment depends on a policy decision regarding the length of the amortization schedule that is separable from the fundamental question of whether the current defined-benefit system is a cost-effective vehicle for delivering retirement benefits to military personnel and their survivors.

APPENDIX C: LEGISLATIVE HISTORY OF COST SHARING IN TRICARE

Patients in TRICARE, the military health care program, generally pay smaller shares of the costs of their care than do participants in most employment-based insurance plans. In recent years, lawmakers have blocked the attempts by the Department of Defense (DoD) to increase cost sharing by patients in an effort to control the costs of the program.

The fee for enrolling in TRICARE Prime (which operates like a health maintenance organization) charged to military retirees who are not yet eligible for Medicare was fixed at $230 per year for individual service members and at $460 per year for families from 1995 until October 1, 2011, when the fees for new enrollees were raised to $260 and $520, respectively (starting October 1, 2012, all enrollees pay those amounts plus an inflation adjustment). Moreover, out-of-pocket expenses have been reduced over time in two areas. The Floyd D. Spence National Defense Authorization Act (NDAA) for Fiscal Year 2001 (Public Law 106-398, section 752) eliminated outpatient copayments for active-duty family members under TRICARE Prime that had been $6 for the families of junior enlisted personnel (pay grades E-4 and below) and $12 for all others. Section 759 of the same legislation reduced the catastrophic cap (the maximum out-of-pocket liability per family for copayments, cost sharing, and deductibles over the course of a fiscal year) under TRICARE Standard from $7,500 to $3,000 for retirees, survivors, and former spouses.

At various times, DoD has proposed increasing out-of-pocket costs for military retirees who are not yet eligible for Medicare. The first proposal came in February 2006, in the form of a program, Sustain the Benefit, that was part of DoD's budget request for 2007. DoD submitted amended versions of that plan in its budget requests for 2008 and 2009. Several provisions of the 2009 proposal would have affected military retirees who were not yet eligible for Medicare:

- The annual enrollment fee for TRICARE Prime would have increased from $460 per family to an amount between $1,100 and $2,140 (in three tiers, on the basis of the amount of retirement pay) over a three-year adjustment period, and fees thereafter would have been indexed to the annual growth rate in the military's health care costs;

- The charge for office visits would have risen (from $12 to $28), as would various other copayments under TRICARE Prime, and all would be adjusted again for inflation every five years;
- For the first time, annual enrollment fees would be assessed for TRICARE Extra (which operates as a preferred-provider network) and Standard (a traditional fee-for-service plan), which would rise over three years to $150 per family and then be indexed thereafter to the annual growth rate in the military's health care costs; and
- The annual family deductible under TRICARE Standard or Extra would have increased over a three-year period in three tiers as a function of the amount of retirement pay.

All of DoD's Sustain the Benefit proposals were blocked by lawmakers. The 2007 NDAA prohibited, through September 30, 2007, any increases in certain health care charges for military beneficiaries along with any increases in copayments under DoD's retail pharmacy system.[1] In particular, the NDAA contained the following provisions:

- Enrollment fees, deductibles, and copayments paid by retirees, their eligible family members, and their survivors for health care purchased from the private sector were frozen;
- The daily copayment amount was capped at $535 for inpatient care provided at private-sector facilities under TRICARE Standard;
- Premiums for the TRICARE Reserve Select program and the TRICARE Retired Reserve program were frozen; and
- Copayments for 30-day prescriptions filled at retail pharmacies were kept at $3 for generic drugs, $9 for brand-name drugs in the TRICARE formulary, and $22 for drugs not listed in the formulary.

The 2008 NDAA extended those provisions through September 30, 2008, and the 2009 NDAA extended them again through September 30, 2009. [2] DoD's budget requests for 2010 and 2011 did not call for any increase in TRICARE fees, but the 2010 NDAA nonetheless extended, through September 30, 2010, the cap on the copayment for inpatient care under TRICARE Standard.[3] The 2011 NDAA extended, through September 30, 2011, the freeze on enrollment fees, deductibles, and copayments made by retirees, their eligible family members, and their survivors, and it extended the pharmacy copayments that had been established four years before.[4] The freeze on premiums for the TRICARE Reserve Select program has expired; DoD now sets the premium equal to 28 percent of the actuarial cost of coverage, and the department updates the premium annually, in keeping with the program's costs realized during the preceding calendar year.[5] Current law requires beneficiaries enrolled in the TRICARE Retired Reserve program to pay 100 percent of the actuarial cost of their coverage with no government subsidy.[6]

APPENDIX D: WERE MILITARY PERSONNEL PROMISED LOW-COST HEALTH CARE IN RETIREMENT?

Much debate has concerned whether retired military personnel and their families have been promised (and are legally entitled to) low-cost or free health care for life. Military recruiters are said to have promised free lifetime health care in some cases as an inducement to people considering military service. The courts, however, have consistently ruled that any such informal promises do not constitute a contract for the military to provide lifetime health care and that only the Congress and the President could establish such a benefit. In October 2000, lawmakers authorized the TRICARE for Life (TFL) program, which supplements Medicare for military retirees and their family members who are eligible for Medicare and largely eliminates their out-of-pocket medical expenses.[1] In 2011, the Department of Defense (DoD) made accrual payments of $11 billion for TFL, and the department spent an additional sum that the Congressional Budget Office estimates at between $14 billion and $18 billion to provide health care to military retirees and their families who were not yet eligible for Medicare.

Before TFL was created, retirees and their families would lose access to the civilian portion of their TRICARE benefits once they became eligible for Medicare, although they retained the right to obtain in-house care at military treatment facilities (MTFs) when space was available and to fill prescriptions without any copayment at MTF pharmacies.

Specifically, the Dependents' Medical Care Act of 1956 states that retired military personnel "may, upon request, be given medical and dental care in any facility of any uniformed service, subject to the availability of space and facilities and the capabilities of the medical and dental staff."[2] However, DoD has closed several military hospitals over the years—including, for example, three closed on the recommendation of the 1993 Defense Base Closure and Realignment Commission; thus the amount of space available has shrunk somewhat.[3] Some military retirees have argued that when such care is no longer available, the federal government is obliged to purchase care in the civilian sector on behalf of retirees and their families.[4]

In the years leading up to the introduction of TFL, lawmakers addressed military retirees' claims that they had been promised lifetime health care but did not go so far as to authorize any new health care benefits for that group. The National Defense Authorization Act for 1998 (Public Law 105-85), states the following:

(a) Findings.—Congress makes the following findings:

(1) Many retired military personnel believe that they were promised lifetime health care in exchange for 20 or more years of service.

(2) Military retirees are the only Federal Government personnel who have been prevented from using their employer-provided health care at or after 65 years of age.

(3) Military health care has become increasingly difficult to obtain for military retirees as the Department of Defense reduces its health care infrastructure.

(4) Military retirees deserve to have a health care program that is at least comparable with that of retirees from civilian employment by the Federal Government.

(5) The availability of quality, lifetime health care is a critical recruiting incentive for the Armed Forces.

(6) Quality health care is a critical aspect of the quality of life of the men and women serving in the Armed Forces.

(b) SENSE OF THE CONGRESS.— It is the sense of Congress that—

(7) the United States has incurred a moral obligation to provide health care to members and former members of the Armed Forces who are entitled to retired or retainer pay (or its equivalent);

(8) it is, therefore, necessary to provide quality, affordable health care to such retirees; and

(9) Congress and the President should take steps to address the problems associated with the availability of health care for such retirees within two years after the date [November 18, 1997] of the enactment of this Act. [5]

Concurrent with Congressional interest, several parties filed lawsuits against the federal government in an attempt to enforce military retirees' claims that they had been promised lifetime health care. In a case first filed in December 1996 (*Schism and Reinlie v. United States*), the plaintiffs alleged that the federal government had breached its implied-in-fact contracts by requiring the plaintiffs to purchase Medicare Part B (which covers doctors' services, outpatient care, home health services, and certain other medical services) to replace the civilian portion of their military health benefit (the Civilian Health and Medical Program of the Uniformed Services— CHAMPUS—the precursor to TRICARE that reimbursed a portion of the costs of health care that military retirees and their family members purchased from the private sector) once they became eligible for Medicare. That case was settled in November 2002 in the U.S. Court of Appeals for the Federal Circuit. On a vote of nine to four, the court ruled that although military recruiters may have enticed recruits with promises of free lifetime health care, those promises did not bind the military to provide such care; only the Congress could establish such a health care benefit, and it had not done so at the time those promises were made:

> Of course, had Congress legislated that the military secretaries could contract with recruits for specific health care benefits, the situation would be different. However, because Congress (1) has enacted statutes for over 100 years that govern the level and availability of health care benefits for active and retired members of the armed services and their dependents; and (2) has never provided funds for contracts made by the secretary with recruits to grant health care, the inescapable conclusion is that Congress simply did not intend to delegate its authority over health care benefits for military members. Rather, it intended to occupy the entire field. In that context, one cannot reasonably infer that by empowering service secretaries to run their respective departments, Congress was silently authorizing them to grant health care benefits via oral promises to recruits by the service's recruiters.[6]

Toward the end of the six-year period during which *Schism and Reinlie v. United States* was disputed, lawmakers authorized the TFL program. TFL began to offer benefits in 2002.

End Notes for Summary

[1] See Congressional Budget Office, Long-Term Implications of the 2013 Future Years Defense Program (July 2012).

[2] See Congressional Budget Office, Reducing the Deficit: Spending and Revenue Options (March 2011), pp. 80–81.

End Notes

[1] DoD specifies notional housing profiles for various combinations of pay grade and dependency status—for example, for a one-bedroom apartment for an E-4 without dependents or for a two-bedroom townhouse for an E-5 with dependents. See Department of Defense, *A Primer on Basic Allowance for Housing (BAH) For the Uniformed Services, 2011* (January 2011), http:// go.usa.gov/y0Q.

[2] For an online calculator, see Department of Defense, "Regular Military Compensation (RMC) Calculator" (accessed November 8, 2012), http://go.usa.gov/y0P.

[3] The third approach—measuring the savings to the beneficiary— was presented in James E. Grefer, *Comparing Military and Civilian Compensation Packages* (Center for Naval Analyses, March 2008), www.cna.org/research/2008/comparing-military-civilian - compensation-packages. That paper was published in support of another publication; see Department of Defense, *Report of the Tenth Quadrennial Review of Military Compensation*, vol. 2, *Deferred and Noncash Compensation* (July 2008), http://go.usa.gov/y0s.

[4] This perspective is in keeping with some earlier work of the Congressional Budget Office. See the statement of Carla Tighe Murray, Senior Analyst, Congressional Budget Office, before the Subcommittee on Personnel, Senate Committee on Armed Services, *Evaluating Military Compensation* (April 28, 2010); and Congressional Budget Office, letter to the Honorable Steny H. Hoyer concerning an analysis of federal civilian and military compensation (January 20, 2011).

[5] The Defense Health Program is the collection of program elements in DoD's Future Years Defense Program that funds the health care activities of TRICARE, the military health care program.

[6] Department of Veterans Affairs, *Annual Budget Submission (FY2013)* (February 2012), http://go.usa.gov/YPDj.

[7] For alternative definitions of military compensation—also from the budgetary perspective—see Maren Leed, *Keeping Faith: Charting a Sustainable Path for Military Compensation* (Center for Strategic and International Studies, October 2011), http://csis.org/files /publication/111118_Leed_KeepingFaith _WebS.pdf; and Todd Harrison, *Analysis of the FY 2012 Defense Budget* (Center for Strategic and Budgetary Assessments, July 2011), www.csbaonline.org/search/?x=0&y=0&q=Analysis+of +the+Fy+2012+Budget.

[8] See Congressional Budget Office, *Long-Term Implications of the 2013 Future Years Defense Program* (July 2012)

[9] See Congressional Budget Office, *Reducing the Deficit: Spending and Revenue Options* (March 2011), pp. 86–87.

[10] The annual pay raises are tabulated in Charles A. Henning, *Military Pay and Benefits: Key Questions and Answers,* CRS Report for Congress RL33446 (Congressional Research Service, updated May 13, 2011). The pay raise that took effect on January 1, 2007, included an across-the-board increase that matched the 2.2 percent rise in the employment cost index, supplemented by an additional targeted pay raise that ranged from 2.5 percent for E-5s to 5.5 percent for E-9s but delayed until April 1, 2007.

[11] Statement of William J. Carr, Deputy Under Secretary of Defense for Military Personnel Policy, before the Subcommittee on Personnel, Senate Committee on Armed Services (April 28, 2010), http://go.usa.gov/yNp.

[12] See Congressional Budget Office, *Recruiting, Retention, and Future Levels of Military Personnel* (October 2006). During 2005, the Army had an average of 7,000 enlisted soldiers

who were involuntarily kept in the service past their contracted separation dates. Almost all left when their stop-loss orders expired.

[13] See Department of Defense, *Report of the Ninth Quadrennial Review of Military Compensation,* vol. 1 (March 2002), p. 29, http://go.usa.gov/yNv. See also the statement of Carla Tighe Murray, Senior Analyst, Congressional Budget Office, before the Subcommittee on Personnel, Senate Committee on Armed Services, *Evaluating Military Compensation* (April 28, 2010); and Congressional Budget Office, *Evaluating Military Compensation* (June 2007).

[14] RMC does not include tax advantages that arise when a service member declares residence in a state that has an income tax if that state excludes certain types of military pay from taxable income. RMC also excludes other tax benefits, such as the exclusion from federal income tax of many types of pay and bonuses (up to certain limits) if earned in a combat zone. For an explanation, see Department of Defense, "Combat Zone Exclusions" (accessed November 8, 2012), http://go.usa.gov/yNw. For this analysis, CBO has not estimated the magnitude of those tax advantages.

[15] Single enlisted members in their first few years of service may live in barracks and not receive a housing allowance. In earlier work, CBO estimated an imputed value for barracks housing, which was slightly higher than the housing allowance for junior personnel. Substituting that value for the allowance would increase the cash compensation for junior enlisted members, but the increase would be small. See Congressional Budget Office, *Evaluating Military Compensation* (June 2007), p. 13.

[14] RMC does not include tax advantages that arise when a service member declares residence in a state that has an income tax if that state excludes certain types of military pay from taxable income. RMC also excludes other tax benefits, such as the exclusion from federal income tax of many types of pay and bonuses (up to certain limits) if earned in a combat zone. For an explanation, see Department of Defense, "Combat Zone Exclusions" (accessed November 8, 2012), http://go.usa.gov/yNw. For this analysis, CBO has not estimated the magnitude of those tax advantages.

[15] Single enlisted members in their first few years of service may live in barracks and not receive a housing allowance. In earlier work, CBO estimated an imputed value for barracks housing, which was slightly higher than the housing allowance for junior personnel. Substituting that value for the allowance would increase the cash compensation for junior enlisted members, but the increase would be small. See Congressional Budget Office, *Evaluating Military Compensation* (June 2007), p. 13.

[16] Section 616 of the National Defense Authorization Act for Fiscal Year 2012 (P.L. 112-81) instituted the proration of imminent danger pay. Imminent danger pay and hostile fire pay are codified in 37 U.S.C. §310 (2006 & Supp.), Special pay: duty subject to hostile fire or imminent danger.

[17] Sections 611 through 615 of the 2012 NDAA, P.L. 112-81, 125 Stat. 1449–1451.

[18] The 2008 NDAA (P.L. 110-181, 122 Stat. 163) initiated a process under which lawmakers would set caps on broad groups of bonuses and forms of special pay, ceding to DoD the authority to set eligibility criteria and detailed pay levels consistent with those caps. Implementation of that authority is phased in over 10 years from the date of enactment and thus will be completed by January 28, 2018.

[19] Section 602 of the 2000 NDAA (113 Stat. 644), superseded by section 602 of the 2004 NDAA (117 Stat. 1498, 37 U.S.C. §1009 (2006)), Adjustments of monthly basic pay.

[20] That presumption on the part of various groups has been reported by James Hosek, "A Recent History of Military Compensation Relative to Private Sector Compensation," in Department

of Defense, *Report of the Ninth Quadrennial Review of Military Compensation*, vol. 2 (March 2002), p. 65, http://go.usa.gov/yNv.

[21] For example, that view is expressed in Military Officers Association of America, "Military Pay Comparability" (accessed November 8, 2012), www.moaa.org/Main_Menu/Take_Action/

[22] See the statement of Major General Dean Tice, Deputy Assistant Secretary of Defense (Military Personnel Policy), in U.S. House of Representatives, *Department of Defense Appropriations for 1982*, hearings before the Subcommittee on the Department of Defense of the Committee on Appropriations (June 1, 1981); reported in Congressional Budget Office, *What Does the Military "Pay Gap" Mean?* (June 1999), pp. 49–51.

[23] President's Commission on an All-Volunteer Armed Force, *Report of the President's Commission on an All-Volunteer Armed Force* (February 1970).

[24] See the statement of Carla Tighe Murray, Senior Analyst, Congressional Budget Office, before the Subcommittee on Personnel, Senate Committee on Armed Services, *Evaluating Military Compensation* (April 28, 2010); and Congressional Budget Office, *Long-Term Implications of the 2011 Future Years Defense Program* (February 2011), Figure B-1.

[25] DoD's goal of paying at the 70th percentile was first stated in Department of Defense, *Report of the Ninth Quadrennial Review of Military Compensation*, vol. 1 (March 2002), http://go.usa.gov/ yNv; that goal was based on the findings of James Hosek and others, *An Analysis of Pay for Enlisted Personnel* (RAND Corporation, 2001), www.rand.org/pubs/documented_briefings/ DB344.html. The recruiting goals are further explained in Department of Defense, *Report of the Tenth Quadrennial Review of Military Compensation*, vol. 1, *Cash Compensation* (February 2008), pp. 3–5, http://go.usa.gov/VPQ.

[26] See Congressional Budget Office, *Evaluating Military Compensation* (June 2007), pp. 12–13.

[27] James E. Grefer and others, "Military and Civilian Compensation: How Do They Compare?" in Department of Defense, *Report of the Eleventh Quadrennial Review of Military Compensation*, vol. 2, *Supporting Research Papers* (July 2012), http://go.usa.gov/wZl.

[28] See Department of Defense, *Report of the Tenth Quadrennial Review of Military Compensation*, vol. 2, *Deferred and Noncash Compensation* (July 2008), p. xi, http://go.usa.gov/y0s.

[29] See Congressional Budget Office, *Evaluating Military Compensation* (June 2007), p. 7.

[30] See Congressional Budget Office, *Comparing the Compensation of Federal and Private-Sector Employees* (January 2012).

[31] See Congressional Budget Office, *Long-Term Implications of the 2013 Future Years Defense Program* (July 2012), p. 15.

[32] Ibid., p. 4.

[33] See Congressional Budget Office, *Reducing the Deficit: Spending and Revenue Options* (March 2011), pp. 76–77.

[34] The 2007 NDAA (120 Stat. 2259, 10 U.S.C. §1409(b)(2006 & Supp.)) increased the amount in determining the annuity for non-disability retirement from the active military. The multiplier for most active military personnel who retired after December 31, 2006, was reset at 2.5 percent times the years of service credited— without the cap—so that very senior personnel (those with more than 30 years of service) could retire at more than 75 percent and conceivably more than 100 percent of their High-3 basic pay.

[35] Sections 641 through 644 of the 2000 NDAA, P.L. 106-65, 113 Stat. 662–664 (1999).

[36] See Department of Defense, "CSB/REDUX Retirement System" (accessed November 8, 2012), http://go.usa.gov/yRp.

[37] See Department of Defense, "Combat Zone Exclusions" (accessed November 8, 2012), http://go.usa.gov/yR6.

[38] Aline Quester and others, *Retirement Choice: 2011* (Center for Naval Analyses, February 2011), www.cna.org/research/2011/ retirement-choice-2011. That study was first published in 2003 and has been revised periodically since then.

[39] See Department of Defense, "Thrift Savings Plan (TSP)" (accessed November 8, 2012), http://go.usa.gov/yRe.

[40] The elective deferral limit for 2012 is $17,000. However, under section 415(c) of the Internal Revenue Code, military personnel may exceed that limit if they are receiving pay under the combat-zone tax exclusion.

[41] Department of Defense, Office of the Actuary, *Valuation of the Military Retirement System, September 30, 2010* (January 2012), p. 24, http://go.usa.gov/vqZ.

[42] That calculation uses nominal discount rates of 17 percent per year for service members and 3 percent per year for the federal government's borrowing costs. Estimated discount rates for service members are from John T. Warner and Saul Pleeter, "The Personal Discount Rate: Evidence from Military Downsizing Programs," *American Economic Review*, vol. 91, no. 1 (2001), pp. 33–53.

[43] The balance in the Military Retirement Fund is held in special-issue (nonmarketable) U.S. Treasury securities. That balance is an asset for the military retirement system but a liability for the rest of the federal government. Payments from the fund count as federal spending; the accrual contributions and payments from the Treasury to amortize the unfunded liability are intergovernmental transactions that have no net effect on federal outlays.

[44] The quoted normal cost percentages do not include the additional amounts that are attributable to concurrent receipt—the fact that, since 2004, military retirement pay for some retirees is no longer reduced dollar for dollar by the amount of disability compensation those retirees receive from the Department of Veterans Affairs. The 2004 NDAA (P.L. 108-136, 117 Stat. 1515) requires that the Treasury, not DoD, make the accrual payments to fund concurrent receipt. See also Department of Defense, *Valuation of the Military Retirement System, September 30, 2010* (January 2012), p. 27, http://go.usa.gov/vqZ.

[45] Department of Defense, *Valuation of the Military Retirement System, September 30, 2010* (January 2012), p. 30, http://go.usa.gov/vqZ.

[46] See Beth J. Asch and others, *Assessing Compensation Reform: Research in Support of the 10th Quadrennial Review of Military Compensation* (RAND Corporation, 2008), www.rand.org/pubs/ monographs/MG764.html. That report supports the policy options explored in Department of Defense, *Report of the Tenth Quadrennial Review of Military Compensation*, vol. 2, *Deferred and Noncash Compensation* (July 2008), http://go.usa.gov/y0s. For a more recent policy proposal, see Defense Business Board, *Modernizing the Military Retirement System*, Report FY11-05 (October 2011), http://go.usa.gov/ynF.

[47] Department of Defense, *Fiscal Year 2013 Budget Request: Overview* (February 2012), p. 5-5, http://go.usa.gov/ynJ.

[48] Department of Defense, *Evaluation of the TRICARE Program: Access, Cost, and Quality, Fiscal Year 2012 Report to Congress* (February 2012), p. 16, http://go.usa.gov/de7.

[49] Those contracts represent a consolidation over time from 10 contracts originally. The first was awarded to Foundation Health Federal Services in March 1995 to cover Washington, Oregon, and six counties in northern Idaho. By June 1998, the entire country was under one contract or another.

[50] Department of Defense, *Evaluation of the TRICARE Program: Access, Cost, and Quality, Fiscal Year 2012 Report to Congress* (February 2012), p. 78, http://go.usa.gov/de7. An independent source shows amounts similar to those estimated by DoD and reported here; see Kaiser Family Foundation and Health Research and Educational Trust, *Employer Health Benefits: 2011 Annual Survey* (September 2011), http://ehbs.kff.org/pdf/2011/8225.pdf. According to that report, the average employee's share of a family HMO premium was $4,148 in 2011 (p. 76). The average annual deductible among HMO plans with an aggregate family deductible (as opposed to plans with separate amounts for each family member and a limit on the number of family members required to reach that amount) was $1,487 (p. 106). The latter amount only approximates DoD's estimate of $980 that the average family paid toward its deductible and copayments because some families do not reach the annual deductible whereas others surpass it.

[51] Department of Defense, *Evaluation of the TRICARE Program: Access, Cost, and Quality, Fiscal Year 2012 Report to Congress* (February 2012), pp. 62, 67, and 72, http://go.usa.gov/de7.

[52] See W. Manning and others, "Health Insurance and the Demand for Medical Care: Evidence from a Randomized Experiment," *American Economic Review*, vol. 77, no. 3 (1987), pp. 251–277; and R. Brook and others, "Does Free Care Improve Adults' Health? Results from a Randomized Controlled Trial," *New England Journal of Medicine*, vol. 309, no. 23 (1983), pp. 1426–1434.

[53] Department of Defense, *Evaluation of the TRICARE Program: Access, Cost, and Quality, Fiscal Year 2012 Report to Congress* (February 2012), pp. 76–77, http://go.usa.gov/de7.

[54] Ibid., p. 80. Again, similar amounts were reported elsewhere. See Kaiser Family Foundation and Health Research and Educational Trust, *Employer Health Benefits: 2011 Annual Survey* (September 2011), http://ehbs.kff.org/pdf/2011/8225.pdf. According to that source, the average employee's share of a family PPO premium was $4,072 in 2011 (p. 76). The average annual deductible among PPO plans with an aggregate family deductible (as opposed to plans with separate amounts for each family member and a limit on the number of family members required to reach that amount) was $1,521 (p. 106), which approximates DoD's estimate of $1,360 in deductibles and copayments.

[55] Sections 712 and 713 of the Floyd D. Spence National Defense Authorization Act for Fiscal Year 2001 (P.L. 106-398, 114 Stat. 1654A–176).

[56] Department of Defense, *TRICARE Pharmacy Program Handbook* (September 2011), http://go.usa.gov/YEeF.

[57] Department of Defense, *Evaluation of the TRICARE Program: Access, Cost, and Quality, Fiscal Year 2012 Report to Congress* (February 2012), p. 82, http://go.usa.gov/de7.

[58] Department of Defense, Defense Health Program, *Fiscal Year (FY) 2013 Budget Estimates, Operation and Maintenance, Procurement, Research, Development, Test and Evaluation*, vol. 1, *Justification of Estimates* (February 2012), pp. 16 and 56–57, http://go.usa.gov/ p5q; and Department of Defense, *Fiscal Year 2013 Budget Request, Overview* (February 2012), p. 5-2, http://go.usa.gov/ynJ.

[59] The Uniformed Services Family Health Plan, a variant of TRICARE Prime, is available to family members of active-duty service members and to military retirees and their family members in six narrowly defined geographic regions.

[60] Department of Defense, *Fiscal Year 2013 Budget Request: Overview* (February 2012), pp. 5-2 to 5-5, http://go.usa.gov/ynJ.

[61] See H. Res. 661, National Defense Authorization Act for Fiscal Year 2013, Section 4501 (passed on May 17, 2012).

[62] The DoD growth rates are from Congressional Budget Office, *Long-Term Implications of the 2013 Future Years Defense Program* (July 2012), pp. 20–23. The economywide growth rate was reported by the Centers for Medicare and Medicaid Services.

[63] See Congressional Budget Office, *The 2012 Long-Term Budget Outlook* (June 2012), p. 53.

[64] See Congressional Budget Office, *The Effects of Proposals to Increase Cost Sharing in TRICARE* (June 2009), p. 16.

[65] See Congressional Budget Office, *Reducing the Deficit: Spending and Revenue Options* (March 2011), pp. 78–81.

End Notes for Appendix A

[1] Sections 641 through 644 of the 2000 NDAA (P.L. 106-65, 113 Stat. 662–664 (1999)).

[2] 10 U.S.C. §1451 (2006 & Supp.).

[3] 10 U.S.C. §12731 (2006 & Supp.).

[4] The rules for concurrent receipt have been relaxed successively in section 636 of the 2003 NDAA (P.L. 107-314, 10 U.S.C. §1413a (2006)), as amended by section 642 of the 2004 NDAA (P.L. 108-136, 117 Stat. 1516) and section 641 of the 2008 NDAA (P.L. 110-181, 122 Stat. 156).

[5] P.L. 108-136, codified at 10 U.S.C. §1466(b)(2)(D), Payments into the [Military Retirement] Fund.

[6] Department of Defense, *Valuation of the Military Retirement System, September 30, 2010* (January 2012), p. 30, http://go.usa.gov/vqZ.

[7] 120 Stat 2259, 10 U.S.C. §1409(b) (2006 & Supp.).

End Notes for Appendix B

[1] Department of Defense, *DoD Financial Management Regulation*, DoD 7000.14-R, Volume 4, Chapter 10, http://go.usa.gov/YEu5.

[2] 10 U.S.C. §1461 (2006 & Supp.), Establishment and purpose of [Military Retirement] Fund; definition.

[3] Section 641 of the National Defense Authorization Act for Fiscal Year 2004 (Public Law 108-136, 117 Stat. 1515), codified at 10 U.S.C. §1466(b)(2)(D) (2006 & Supp.), Payments into the [Military Retirement] Fund.

[4] Department of Defense, *Valuation of the Military Retirement System, September 30, 2010* (January 2012), p. 24, http://go.usa.gov/vqZ.

[5] Ibid., p. 25.

[6] Ibid., p. 30.

[7] Defense Business Board, *Modernizing the Military Retirement System,* Report FY11-05 (October 2011), Tab C, pp. 10 and 20, http://go.usa.gov/ynF.

End Notes for Appendix C

[1] Section 704 of the 2007 NDAA (P.L. 109-364, 120 Stat. 2280– 2284).

[2] Sections 701 and 702 of the 2008 NDAA, P.L. 110–181, 122 Stat. 187 and 122, Stat. 188; and sections 701 and 702 of the 2009 NDAA, P.L. 110–417, 122 Stat. 4498.

[3] Section 709 of the 2010 NDAA, P.L. 111–84, 123 Stat. 2378.

[4] Sections 701 and 705 of the 2011 NDAA, P.L. 111–383, 124 Stat. 4244 and 124 Stat. 4246.

[5] 10 U.S.C. §1076d(d)(3) (2006 & Supp.). For information, see "Your Profile: TRICARE Reserve Select" (July 25, 2012), http://go.usa.gov/mEk.

[6] See "Your Profile: TRICARE Retired Reserve" (July 25, 2012), http://go.usa.gov/mE0.

End Notes for Appendix D

[1] Sections 712 and 713 of the Floyd D. Spence National Defense Authorization Act (NDAA) for Fiscal Year 2001 (Public Law 106- 398, 114 Stat. 1654A-176).

[2] Ch. 374, 70 Stat. 250, 253; codified at 10 U.S.C. §1074(b)(1) (2006 & supp.), Medical and dental care for members and certain former members.

[3] The 1993 commission's recommendations led to the closing of the naval hospitals in Charleston, South Carolina; Oakland, California; and Orlando, Florida. See *Defense Base Closure and Realignment Commission: 1993 Report to the President*, http://go.usa.gov /YEJ4.

[4] For a comprehensive review of these issues through 2005, see David F. Burrelli, *Military Health Care: The Issue of "Promised" Benefits,* CRS Report for Congress 98-1006 (Congressional Research Service, updated January 19, 2006).

[5] Section 752 of the 1998 NDAA, P.L. 105-85 (111 Stat. 1823).

[6] *Schism and Reinlie v. United States*, 316 F.3d 1259, 1271 (Fed.Cir. (2002)).

In: Military Pay and Benefits
Editor: Walter Avraham

Chapter 2

MILITARY PAY AND BENEFITS: KEY QUESTIONS AND ANSWERS*

Charles A. Henning

SUMMARY

From the earliest days of the republic, America's Armed Forces have been compensated by military pay, commonly known as "basic pay." While the original pay structure was quite simple and straightforward, over time a complex system of pay, allowances, incentives, and bonuses has evolved.

With the advent of the all-volunteer force in 1973, Congress has used military pay and its associated allowances to improve recruiting, retention, and the overall quality of the force. Congress, in the National Defense Authorization Act, typically authorizes military pay adjustments for the coming fiscal year. Today's ongoing military operations in Iraq and Afghanistan, combined with concern over government spending and the debt ceiling, suggest that further changes in pay, allowances, incentives, and bonuses will continue to receive congressional scrutiny.

In the nearly 10 years since the terrorist attacks of September 11, 2001, basic pay has increased nominally by nearly 35% (figure not adjusted for inflation). This figure does not include other increases in allowances, bonuses, or incentives. The cumulative effect is that most

---

* This is an edited, reformatted and augmented version of a Congressional Research Service publication, CRS Report for Congress RL33446, from www.crs.gov, prepared for Members and Committees of Congress, dated May 13, 2011.

analysts now agree that the average annual cost per servicemember exceeds $100,000.

Many observers are currently concerned about the cost of recent manpower increases, the impact of personnel costs on the overall defense budget, and the potential decrement to equipment modernization plans caused by the increased pressure of the personnel account. To date, however, it appears that the increasing cost of personnel has not come at the expense of other elements in the defense budget.

The issue of pay comparability between military and civilian pay, commonly referred to as the "pay gap," continues to receive emphasis. Advocates for higher pay have emphasized the sacrifices being made today by the American military, the high personnel tempo and reduced dwell time, the impact on families caused by frequent deployments, and the positive impact that raises have had on recruiting and retention. Others argue that the "pay gap" is an imprecise measurement that does not fully account for other compensation increases in the form of allowances, incentives, and bonuses. Still others believe that the military is already better compensated than their civilian counterparts, especially during this period of high unemployment.

The Department of Defense (DOD), on the other hand, bases its recommendations regarding military pay on its own standard for pay comparability. The DOD standard establishes that members should be compensated at the 70th percentile of wages for civilian employees with similar levels of education, age, experience, and responsibility.

This report addresses the role of military pay in manning the Armed Forces, the types of pay increases used in the past, recent reforms in managing pay, and the role of the Employment Cost Index in determining basic pay increases. The report also reviews the compensation benefits specifically available to military personnel participating in Operation Iraqi Freedom (OIF)/Operation New Dawn (OND) and Operation Enduring Freedom (OEF).

INTRODUCTION

All servicemembers are entitled to one primary form of compensation, which is commonly referred to as "basic pay."[1] The amount of pay received is based on rank (also referred to as Pay Grade) and longevity. Promotions result in increased compensation with additional longevity pay increases occurring every two years on a range of "Under 2" to "Over 38." In addition to base pay, there are a number of allowances, bonuses, and incentives designed to attract and retain quality personnel with the right skills.

Since the advent of the all-volunteer military in 1973 and particularly over the past 10 years, Congress has used military compensation to improve the recruiting, retention, and overall quality of the force. This has been particularly important for the Army, which missed its annual recruiting target of 80,000 by 6,627 soldiers in FY2005 and struggled to meet the same mission requirement in FY2006 and FY2007.

In the nearly 10 years since the terrorist attacks of September 11, 2001, basic pay has been nominally increased by nearly 35% (figure not adjusted for inflation).

This figure does not include other increases in allowances, bonuses, or incentives. The cumulative effect is that most analysts now agree that the average annual cost per servicemember exceeds $100,000.

While these pay increases have been significant, veterans' support organizations have continued to emphasize the importance of closing the "pay gap" to ensure that servicemembers are compensated at the same level as their civilian counterparts. There is, however, no consensus among analysts on how the pay gap should be defined or measured. This results in multiple options for calculating any pay gap. By one commonly used measure, the FY2011 pay raise will close the pay gap of servicemembers lagging behind civilians to an estimated 2.4%.

One of the common concerns expressed today is that recent strength increases in the Army and Marine Corps with the resulting increase in the cost of the personnel account will begin to impact on the equipment modernization plans of the services.

Today's ongoing military operations in Iraq and Afghanistan, combined with concern over government spending and the debt ceiling, suggest that future changes in pay, allowances, incentives, and bonuses will continue to receive congressional scrutiny.

KEY QUESTIONS AND ANSWERS

1. Why Did the Adequacy of Active Duty Military Pay Become a Major Issue Beginning in the Late 1990s?

Since the end of the draft in 1972-1973, the "adequacy" of military pay has tended to become an issue for Congress for one or both of two reasons: if it appears that

- the military services are having trouble recruiting enough new personnel, or keeping sufficient career personnel, of requisite quality; or

- the standard of living of career personnel is perceived to be less fair or equitable than that which demographically comparable civilians (in terms of age, education, skills, responsibilities, and similar criteria) can maintain.

The first issue is an economic inevitability on at least some occasions. In the absence of a draft, the services must compete in the labor market for new enlistees and—a fact often overlooked— have always had to compete in the labor market for more mature individuals to staff the career force. There are always occasions when unemployment is low, and hence recruiting is more difficult, and others when unemployment is high and military service a more attractive alternative.

The second situation, while often triggered by the first, is frequently stated in moral or ethical terms. Proponents of this viewpoint argue that, even if quantitative indexes of recruiting and retention appear to be satisfactory, the crucial character of the military's mission of national defense, and its acceptance of the professional ethic that places survival below mission accomplishment, demands certain levels of compensation. Beginning in the mid-1990s, several new factors caused recruiting and retention problems severe enough to move Congress once again to deal with this issue.

Among the factors cited by analysts were (1) a public impression that the end of the Cold War meant that military service was no longer interesting, relevant, or even viable as a career option; (2) the post-Cold War drawdown in active duty military manpower by 40%, which greatly reduced real and perceived enlistment and career retention opportunities; (3) the 1990s economic expansion, which led to the explosive growth of actual and perceived civilian career options; (4) a rise in civilian consumer living standards against which military families measure their own economic success or failure; (5) concerns over increased family separation due to more operations and training away from home, whether "home" was in the United States or in foreign countries; (6) a decreased propensity for military service among young people for other reasons, such as anti-military parents and educators; (7) skepticism about new missions such as "operations other than war," "peacekeeping," or "peace enforcement"; and (8) the availability of government educational assistance from other sources ("the GI Bill without the GI").

2. What Kinds of Increases in Military Pay and Benefits Have Been Considered or Used in the Past?

Many military compensation analysts have strongly criticized across-the-board rather than selective pay raises. They argue that across-the-board increases fail to bring resources to bear where they are most needed. Percentage increases targeted on particular pay grades and number of years of service and special pays and bonuses targeted on particular occupational skills, they suggest, would maximize the recruiting and retention gains for the compensation dollars spent. Across-the-board increases also affect a variety of other costs; retired pay, for instance, is computed as a percentage of basic pay.

The services already do a great deal of such targeting, having maintained a large system of special pays and bonuses since the end of conscription over 35 years ago. Personnel managers report no indication that such targeted compensation has had the deleterious effects on morale and cohesion that some had feared. Across-the-board pay increases, however, are believed by many to have the advantages of simplicity, visibility, and equity. If everyone gets a similar percentage increase, nobody can feel, or can claim, that he or she has been left out. It also shows up immediately, in the person's next paycheck, rather than months or years later when a particular individual is next eligible for a lump sum special pay or bonus (some special pays and bonuses are paid monthly or biweekly, as part of regular pay). It is likely that, as in the past, overall increases in military cash compensation over the next several years will combine both across-the-board and targeted increases. Both of these increases, because of their broad appeal, may well be sound approaches to improving recruiting and retention as much as possible. In addition, many observers believe that the recent enactment of the new Post 9/11 GI Bill benefit with its generous benefits and transferability options will have an overall beneficial impact on both recruiting and retention.

Recruiting and retention problems are not necessarily solved by increasing military pay. Many components of the military compensation system that are important to recruiting and retention efforts, especially the latter, do not involve cash pay. These include retirement benefits; health care; housing; permanent change of station (PCS) moving costs and policies; exchanges, commissaries, and other retail facilities; and recreational facilities. A wide range of views about existing military personnel management practices suggests that the services' requirements for both new enlistees and career people could be significantly reduced by changing often longstanding and inter-related assignment, promotion, career development, or retirement policies. Survey research also reveals that the sense of patriotism, public service, and *esprit de corps* found in capable and combat-ready Armed Forces is extremely significant to both new enlistees and career members.

Furthermore, there are always limits to what increased compensation, whether cash or in-kind, can do to help any organization cope with personnel difficulties. Job and career satisfaction; public and elite views of the importance and legitimacy of the military as an institution; unit morale; and success in operational deployments and especially in combat may well be independent of compensation variables. High "scoring" in these intangibles, especially for a unique organization and culture like the Armed Forces, can and frequently does balance perceived issues in compensation. However, few analysts believe that recruiting and retention rates can be sustained at the necessary levels without continuing to maintain the momentum of recent pay raises. Many long-time observers seem to feel that money alone cannot keep a person in the military for a full career if the person does not like the military culture; they assert that the lifestyle is too demanding and too arduous for most. At the same time, it is argued that people can be driven out of the military if their compensation and living standards are not at least somewhat close to those of their demographic and educational counterparts in civilian life.

3. What Is "Pay Table Reform"?

The military pay table displays the amount of monthly basic pay which a servicemember is entitled to based on the member's pay grade[2] and length of service. Until 2007, the length of service component of the table ranged from "under 2" to "over 26" years of service and provided an incremental longevity pay raise every two years.[3] As a result, servicemembers received their final longevity raise at 26 years of service even though their rank may have provided for service to or beyond 30 years. This pay table changed very little since it was introduced in 1958.[4] Some analysts advocated longer military careers rather than the current emphasis on youth and vigor and argued that the pay tables should be extended or "reformed" to allow for service beyond 30 years with continuing longevity increases. This was commonly referred to as the "40- year" pay table. The FY2007 John Warner National Defense Authorization Act (NDAA) included several significant changes to the pay table. First, effective April 1, 2007, the pay table was extended from "over 26" to "over 40" years of service.[5] Second, and also effective April 1, 2007, the

NDAA provided additional longevity increases at 30, 34, and 38 years of service for the most senior enlisted, warrant officer, and officer pay grades.[6] For example, the final longevity raise for E-8, W-4, 0-6, and 0-7 will occur at "over 30" years; at "over 34" for pay grades E-8, W-5, and 0- 8; and at "over 38" for pay grades 0-9 and 0-10. Third, effective January 1, 2007, the NDAA provides additional retirement credit for service beyond 30 years, continuing to accrue at the rate of 2.5% per year.[7] As a result, a servicemember who retires with 40 years of service will now qualify for 100% of basic pay in their retirement. The cumulative effect of these changes seems to suggest congressional support for longer military careers. However, the NDAA did not address other cited constraints to facilitating longer careers. Specifically, there were no changes to mandatory retirement based on years of service or age and no increase in the percentage of E-8, E-9, and W-5 who may be on active duty at a given time. As a result, the beneficiaries of this change are the most senior enlisted, warrant, and officer personnel who will continue to receive longevity pay raises and retirement credit beyond the traditional 30-year point.

4. How Are Each Year's Increases in Military Pay Computed? Definitions

The across-the-board increases in military pay discussed each year relate to military basic pay. Basic pay is the one element of military compensation that all military personnel in the same pay grade and with the same number of years of service receive. Basic allowance for housing, or BAH, is received by military personnel not living in military housing, either family housing or barracks. Basic allowance for subsistence, or BAS, is the cost of meals. All servicemembers receive BAS but at different rates based on officer or enlisted status. A federal income tax advantage accrues because the BAH and BAS allowances are not subject to federal income tax. Basic pay, BAH, BAS, and the federal income tax advantage all comprise what is known as Regular Military Compensation (RMC). RMC is that index of military pay which tends to be used most often in comparing military with civilian compensation; analyzing the standards of living of military personnel; and studying military compensation trends over time, or by service geographical area, or skill area. Basic pay is between 65% and 75% of RMC, depending on individual circumstances. RMC specifically *excludes* all special pays and bonuses, reimbursements, educational assistance, deferred compensation (i.e., an economic valuation of future retired pay), or any estimate of the cash value of non-monetary benefits such as health care or military retail stores.[8]

Annual Percentage Increases in Military Basic Pay

Military Basic Pay Raises Linked to Employment Cost Index (ECI) Percentage Increases

Permanent law (37 USC. 1009) provides that monthly basic pay is to be increased by the annual percentage increase in the Employment Cost Index (ECI). For fiscal years 2004, 2005, and 2006, the law required the military raise to be equal to the ECI increase plus an additional one half percentage point (i.e., if the ECI annual increase were to be 3.0%, the military raise would be 3.5%).

The ECI, calculated by the Department of Labor's Bureau of Labor Statistics, measures annual percentage increases in wages, salaries, and employer costs for employee benefits on all private-sector employees, although it can be subdivided to measure increases in specific categories of such employees.

Indexing the annual military pay raise to the annual increase in the ECI was established by Sec. 602 of the FY2004 NDAA (P.L. 108-136, November 24, 2003; 117 Stat. 1498, amending 37 USC. 1009). Previously, the annual military pay raise was linked to the annual percentage increases in the General Schedule (GS) federal civil service pay scale.

Congress Usually Sets the Amount of the Military Pay Raise

Despite the statutory formula, which could operate each year without any further action, Congress has legislated a particular percentage increase in military pay every year since 1980, with the exception of 1982 and 2011. During the period 1982-1999, the percentage increase in military pay was usually identical to that granted to GS civilians.

The only exceptions during this period were 1985 and 1994, when Congress provided larger increases in military pay. Even with the 2004 introduction of the Employment Cost Index as the single index for military pay, Congress has, in most cases, explicitly reiterated the increase in law rather than deferring to the permanent statutory formula. Therefore, while Congress may legislate the military pay raise percentage, the operation of the permanent formula remains important in determining what the percentage will actually be.

Annual Increases in Basic Allowances for Housing (BAH) and Subsistence (BAS)

Housing (37 USC. 403) and subsistence (37 USC. 402) allowances are paid to all personnel not living in military housing or eating in military dining facilities or using field rations. Monthly BAH varies by rank, by whether the person has dependents, and, most importantly, by location. BAS, on the other hand, is paid at a uniform rate to all officers and at a uniform but slightly higher rate for all enlisted personnel.

Annual increases in BAH and BAS are both based on surveys of local housing and food costs respectively, and thus are not affected by the annual percentage increase in the ECI. (For many years BAH and its predecessors and BAS were subject to the annual percentage increase; this was not changed until the late 1990s.)

There have been occasional proposals to survey the housing costs on which BAH is based more frequently than once a year, due to rapidly rising housing costs in many areas of the United States. Particular emphasis is placed by supporters of more frequent surveys on fast-rising electricity costs, notably for heating and cooling.

In addition, there have been calls to merge BAS with basic pay to reduce the complexity of military compensation and the need for BAS computations each year.

5. What Have Been the Annual Percentage Increases in Active Duty Military Basic Pay Since 1993 (FY1994)? What Were Each Year's Major Executive and Legislative Branch Proposals and Actions on the Annual Percentage Increase in Military Basic Pay?

The following subsections itemize action on the active duty military basic pay increase going back to 1993 (the FY1994 budget). *Unless otherwise noted, all increases were proposed to be effective on January 1 of the fiscal year indicated. The same is true of discussions of future pay raises.*

2010 (FY2011). Statutory formula: 1.4%. Administration request:1.4%. The House version of the FY2011 NDAA supported a 1.9% across-the-board pay raise; a raise 0.5% above the ECI. Both the Senate-reported bill and H.R. 6523 (the House and Senate-passed version of the NDAA) were silent on the pay raise issue. As a result, 37 USC. 1009 became operative with an automatic January 1, 2011, across-the-board raise of 1.4%; equal to the ECI. At 1.4%, this was the smallest military pay raise since 1962, when no raise was enacted. *Final version:* 1.4% across-the-board.

2009 (FY2010). Statutory formula: 2.9%. *Administration request:* 2.9%. *Final version:* 3.4% across-the-board (0.5% higher than the ECI) effective January 1, 2010.

2008 (FY2009). Statutory formula: 3.4%. *Administration request:* 3.4%. *Final version:* 3.9% across-the-board increase (0.5% higher than the annual ECI increase).

2007 (FY2008). Statutory formula: 3.0%. *Administration request:* 3.0% across-the-board. *Final version:* 3.5% across-the-board. The presidential veto of the initial FY2008 NDAA resulted in a 3.0% pay raise taking effect on January 1, 2008 (statutory formula), with the remaining 0.5% being made retroactive to January 1, 2008, upon enactment of the final version of the FY2008 NDAA (H.R. 4986; P.L. 110-181).

2006 (FY2007). Statutory formula: 2.2%. Under current law, the FY2007 pay was based solely on the ECI and not a rate 0.5% higher than the ECI. *Administration request:* 2.2% across the board. *Final Version:* 2.2% across the board but with an additional April 1, 2007, targeted pay raise that would be as high as 8.3% for some warrant officers and range from 2.5% for E-5s to 5.5% for E-9s.[9]

2005 (FY2006). Statutory formula: 3.1%. (0.5% higher than the annual increase in the Employment Cost Index (ECI) which was 2.6%). *Administration request:* 3.1% across-the-board. *Final version:* 3.1% across the board.

2004 (FY2005). Statutory formula: 3.5%. *Administration request:* 3.5% across-the-board. *Final version*: FY2005 NDAA (Section 601, P.L. 108-375, October 28, 2004; 118 Stat. 1811), 3.5% across-the-board. [Unlike the years 1999-2003 (FY2000-FY2004), the Administration did not request and the Congress did not enact, a "targeted" increase based on which particular pay grades and years-of-service cohorts need more pay to improve career retention.]

2003 (FY2004). Statutory formula: 3.7%. *Administration request:* Average 4.1%; minimum 2.0%; maximum of 6.5%. *Final version.* FY2004 NDAA (Section 601, P.L. 108-136, November 24, 2003; 117 Stat. 1392). Average 4.15%: floor 3.7%; maximum 6.25% for some senior NCOs. Also included language requiring that after FY2006, the annual military pay raise would be equal to the annual percentage rise in the Employment Cost Index (see above, #3, for a description of the ECI), thus repealing previous law that had the effect of mandating a pay raise equal to the ECI *minus* 0.5%. Existing temporary law, enacted in 1999 in the FY2000 NDAA, which required an increase equal to the ECI plus 0.5% during FY2001-FY2006, was not changed. (See below under "Suspension of Statutory Formula during FY2001-FY2006.)

2002 (FY2003). Statutory formula: 4.1%. *Administration request:* Minimum 4.1%; average 4.8%; for some mid-level and senior noncommissioned officers, warrant officers, and mid-level commissioned officers, between 5.0% and 6.5%. *Final increase:* identical to the Administration request, embodied, as usual, in the FY2003 Bob Stump National Defense Authorization Act (P.L. 107-314, December 2, 2002; 116 Stat. 2458). The House and Senate had also approved the Administration request.

2001 (FY2002). Statutory formula: 4.6%. *Administration request:* numerous figures for the "Administration request" were mentioned in the pay raise debate, depending on when and which agency produced the figures.

In general, however, they all proposed increases of at least 5% and no more than 15% (the latter applying only to a very few individuals), depending on pay grade and years of service; the average increase for FY2002 was 6.9%. *Final increase:*

Eventually, the FY2002 National Defense Authorization Act (Section 601, P.L. 107-107, December 28, 2001) endorsed an "Administration request" of between 5 and 10%, depending on pay grade and years of service. These increases remain the largest across-the-board percentage raises since that of FY1982, which took effect on October 1, 1981. The latter was a 14.3% across-the-board raise, which followed an 11.7% raise the previous year, FY1981, resulting in a two-year raise of almost 28%. This was principally in response to the high inflation of the late 1970s.

2000 (FY2001). Statutory formula: 3.7% (based on the 1999/FY2000 legislation; the original statutory formula would have led to a proposed raise of 2.7%). *Administration request:* 3.7%. *Final increase:* The FY2001 Floyd D. Spence National Defense Authorization Act (Section 601, P.L. 106-398, October 30, 2000; 114 Stat. 1654A-1 at A-143) approved the 3.7% figure. In addition, as was the case in the previous year, additional increases averaging 0.4% (based on the size of the across-the-board raise the amount of money used would have funded; the range of additional percentage raises was between 1.0 and 5.5%) were provided to middle-grade officer and enlisted personnel, to be effective July 1, 2001.

1999 (FY2000). Statutory formula: 4.8%. *Administration request:* 4.4% on January 1, 2000, but in addition, on July 1, 2000, a wide range of targeted increases averaging an additional 1.4% (again, based on the size of across-the-board raise the cost of the targeted increases would finance) in mid-level officer and enlisted grades' pay levels.

Final increase: The FY2000 National Defense Authorization Act (Section 601, P.L. 106-65; October 5, 1999) raised the January 1, 2000, increase to 4.8%, and accepted the July 1, 2000, targeted increases.

1998 (FY1999). Statutory formula: 3.1%. *Administration request:* 3.6%. The House approved 3.6%, or whatever percentage increase was approved for federal GS civilians, whichever was higher. The Senate approved 3.6%. *Final increase:*

The FY1999 Strom Thurmond National Defense Authorization Act (Section 601, P.L. 105-261; October 17, 1998; 112 Stat. 1920 at 2036) approved the House alternative, which resulted in a 3.6% military increase, as GS civilians also received 3.6%.

1997 (FY1998). Statutory formula: 2.8%. *Administration request:* 2.8%. *Final increase:* FY1998 National Defense Authorization Act (Section 601, P.L. 105-85, November 18, 1997; 111 Stat. 1629 at 1771): 2.8%.

1996 (FY1997). Statutory formula: 2.3%. *Administration request:* 3.0%. *Final increase:*

The House and Senate both approved the higher Administration request of 3.0%, and it was therefore included in the FY1997 National Defense Authorization Act (Section 601, P.L. 104-201, September 23, 1996; 110 Stat. 2422 at 2539).

1995 (FY1996). Statutory formula: 2.4%. *Administration request:* 2.4%. *Final increase:* Congress also approved 2.4% in the FY1996 National Defense Authorization Act (Section 601, P.L. 104- 106, February 10, 1996; 110 Stat. 186 at 356).

1994 (FY1995). Statutory formula: 2.6%. *Administration request:* 1.6%; one percent less than the statutory formula. *Final increase:* The FY1995 National Defense Authorization Act (Section 601, P.L. 103-337, October 5, 1994; 108 Stat. 2663 at 2779) authorized the statutory formula figure of 2.6%.

1993 (FY1994). Statutory formula: 2.2%. *Administration request:* No increase; military (and civil service) pay would have been frozen in FY1994. The Administration also proposed limiting future civil service—and hence active duty military—pay raises to one percentage point less than that provided by the existing statutory formula. None of these proposals was adopted. *Final increase:*

The FY1994 National Defense Authorization Act (Section 601, P.L. 103-160, November 30, 1993, 107 Stat. 1547 at 1677) authorized 2.2%.

6. Is There a "Pay Gap" Between Military and Civilian Pay, So That Generally Military Pay Is Less than That of Comparable Civilians? If So, What Is the Extent of the "Gap"?

The issue of a military-civilian "pay gap" raises several questions:

- How can the existence of a gap be determined and the gap be measured?
- Is there a gap, with civilians or the military being paid more? If so, how much of a gap?
- If there is a gap, does that in itself require action?
- What are the effects of any such gaps?

A wide range of studies over the past several decades has compared military and civilian (both federal civil service and private sector) compensation.

In general, the markedly different ways in which civilian public and private sector compensation and benefit systems are structured, compared to that of the Armed Forces, make it difficult to validate any generalizations about whether there is a "gap" between military and civilian pay. Some advocates for federal civil servants argue that federal civilian pay lags behind private sector pay, which in turn leads some people, given the past linkage between civil service and military pay percentage increases, to infer that military pay lags behind private sector pay. However, because the current statistic used to measure private sector pay, the ECI, measures annual percentage increases and not dollar amounts, no such inference is really possible.

As noted above, the debate, in recent years, over "pay parity" between the military and federal civil service pay increases, involves the percentage amount of the civilian pay raise. It has not, so far, involved the military pay raise proposal at all.

The issue has been whether the civil service should get a percentage raise identical to that of the military, or whether the military should get a higher raise because of (1) the much greater degree of danger and hardship military service entails, compared to most civilian employment, especially in time of war, and (2) the need to cope with actual or forestall potential military recruiting and retention problems.

Measuring and Confirming a "Gap"

It is extremely difficult to find a common index or indicator to compare the dollar values of military and civilian compensation. First, military compensation includes numerous separate components, whose receiving population and taxability vary widely. Which of these, if any, should be included in a military-civilian pay comparison? Furthermore, total military compensation includes a wide range of non-monetary benefits: a retirement annuity after "vesting" at 20 years of service, health care, retail stores, and recreational facilities. Few civilians work in organizations where analogous benefits are provided. Attempts to facilitate a comparison by assigning a cash value to non-cash benefits almost always founder on the large number of debatable assumptions that must be made to generate such an estimate.

Second, it is also extremely difficult to establish a comparison between military ranks and pay grades on the one hand, and civilian jobs on the other. The range of knowledge, supervision, and professional judgment required of military personnel and civilians performing similar duties in a standard peacetime industrial or office milieu may well be similar. When the same military member's likely job in the field, possibly in combat, is concerned, comparisons become difficult.

Third, generally speaking, with some exceptions, the conditions of military service are frequently much more arduous than those of civilian employment, even in peacetime, for families as well as military personnel themselves. This aspect of military service is sometimes cited as a rationale for military compensation being at a higher level than it otherwise might be. On the other hand, the military services all mention travel and adventure in exotic places as a positive reason for enlistment and/or a military career, so it may be misleading to automatically assume this is always a liability.

Fourth, comparisons between different sets of compensation statistics, and the use of these comparisons to determine what military pay should be, can yield very different results. Comparing *dollar amounts* may lead to different conclusions than comparing the *annual increases* in pay for each position. The percentage increase in pay over different time periods is more often than not very different. Different indexes with different components can be used to determine compensation changes.

Finally, the level of specificity used in a pay comparison can lead to sharply differing results, especially when the comparison is between private sector and federal pay as a whole, both civil service and military. For instance, all Army colonels may, according to some indexes, be paid roughly as much as federal civil service GS-15s, or as much as private sector managers with certain responsibilities. Thus, those occupational specialties that are highly paid in the private sector—health care, information technology, some other scientific and engineering skills, are examples—are frequently paid considerably less in the military or in the civil service. Other common subcategories for comparison, in addition to occupational skill, include age, gender, years in the labor force, and educational levels.

As noted by the Congressional Budget Office:[10]

> Comparing compensation in the military and civilian sectors can be problematic. One obvious limitation is that such comparisons cannot easily account for different job characteristics. Many military jobs are more hazardous, require frequent moves, and are less flexible than civilian jobs in the same field. Members of the armed forces are subject to military discipline, are considered to be on duty at all times, and are unable to resign, change jobs at will or negotiate pay. Military personnel also receive extensive training, paid for by the government. Family support programs are generally more available in the military compared with civilian employers. Intangible rewards, such as a shared sense of purpose, may be higher among military personnel as well. Quantifying those elements among military and civilian personnel is extremely difficult.

Estimates of a Military-Civilian Pay Gap

Numerous comparisons of military and civilian compensation in recent years have been cited either to illustrate a gap that favors civilian pay levels or to refute the existence of such a gap. Many of these reports lack precision in identifying what aspects of military pay were compared with civilian pay, which indexes were used to make the comparison, or the length of time covered by the comparison. Although it is difficult to generalize, it would appear that most of those estimates which assert that there is a pay gap in favor of higher civilian pay find a percentage difference of between 2% and 13% in recent years with parity being achieved most recently in 1982. Other analysts, using a slightly different measurement which includes the housing allowance in the calculation, contend that the pay gap vanished in 2002 and that there is currently an 11% military pay surplus.[11]

Estimates have been made that question the existence of a gap favoring civilians. These tend to compare specific populations of military personnel with equally specific subcategories of civilians. Analyses of this nature appear to be less common than the across-the-board comparisons, almost certainly because they are much more difficult to do.[12]

In 2002, General Accounting Office (GAO) analysts itemized the components of the military benefit package—such as military retirement, health care, Servicemembers' Group Life Insurance, base recreational facilities, and the like—and compared them with the private sector. It found that the range of benefits available to military personnel was generally comparable to, and in some cases superior to, benefits available in the private sector. The GAO study did not appear to have made dollar-figure comparisons or compared military non-cash benefits—such as health care, commissaries or exchanges, or annual leave—with benefits in the private sector, either by figuring out their dollar worth or by itemizing their exact provisions in great detail.[13]

This GAO report was followed in 2008 by the 10th Quadrennial Review of Military Compensation (QRMC)[14] which also addressed the pay gap issue and recommended that a new comparative model could be better suited to measuring the difference between military pay and comparable civilian occupations. The commission recommended replacing Regular Military Compensation (RMC) with a new measure called Military Annual Compensation (MAC). While RMC includes base pay, BAH, BAS and the federal tax advantage from the two allowances, MAC would also factor in the health care benefit, the value of the military retirement annuity, and state and Social Security tax advantages. Based on the QRMC analysis and using MAC as the comparative tool, enlisted and officer personnel fare better than their civilian counterparts in cash compensation according to the economic modeling done by the QRMC. This represents the first time that a QRMC has recommended inclusion of benefits when comparing military and civilian compensation levels.

While estimating the pay gap continues to be a challenge, it appears that the substantial increases in military pay and benefits since the late 1990s, whatever the existing relative relationship of military to civilian compensation as of that time, have probably had the effect of favoring the military.

If There Is a Pay Gap, Does It Necessarily Matter?

Some have suggested that the emphasis on a pay gap, whether real or not, or if real, how much, is unwarranted and not a good guide to arriving at sound policy. They argue that the key issue is, or should be, not *comparability* of military and civilian compensation, but the *competitiveness* of the former. Absent a draft, the Armed Forces must compete in the labor market for new enlisted and officer personnel. has always had to compete with civilian opportunities, real or perceived. Given these facts, some ask what difference it makes whether military pay is much lower, the same, or higher than that of civilians? If the services are having recruiting difficulties, then pay increases might be appropriate, even if the existing "gap" favors the military. Conversely, if military compensation is lower than equivalent civilian pay, and if the services are doing well in recruiting and retaining sufficient numbers of qualified personnel, then there might be no reason to raise military pay.

However, some believe that explicitly basing military compensation on "purely economic" competitiveness with civilian pay could have undesirable consequences: for instance, in a time of economic difficulty, the military might be receiving lower pay than most civilians but still recruiting satisfactorily due to high unemployment.

For further discussion of the "pay gap" issue, see Congressional Budget Office, *What Does the Military "Pay Gap" Mean?* June 1999; and Association of the US Army, [A non-profit group that works to advance the interests of military members.] *Closing the Pay Gap*, Arlington, VA, October 2000.

7. What Benefits Are Specifically Available for Military Personnel Participating in Operation Iraqi Freedom (OIF)/Operation New Dawn (OND)[15] and Operation Enduring Freedom (OEF)?[16]

Hostile Fire/Imminent Danger Pay

Many military personnel participating in OEF and OIF/OND may be eligible for Hostile Fire or Imminent Danger Pay (HF/IDP). HF/IDP is authorized by 37 USC. 310, which provides a special pay for "duty subject to hostile fire or imminent danger." While DOD regulations distinguish between Hostile Fire Pay and Imminent Danger Pay, both are derived from the same statute. An individual can only collect Hostile Fire Pay or Imminent Danger Pay, not both simultaneously. The purpose of this pay is to compensate servicemembers for physical danger. Iraq, Afghanistan, Kuwait, Saudi Arabia, and many other nearby countries have been declared imminent danger zones by the Secretary of Defense. Military personnel serving in such designated areas are eligible for HF/IDP. To be eligible for this pay in a given month, a servicemember must have served some time in one of the designated zones, even if only a day or less. The authorizing statute for HF/IDP previously set the rate at $150 per month. However, the FY2004 National Defense Authorization Act (NDAA) (P.L. 108-136, section 619) temporarily increased this rate to $225, through December 31, 2004. The FY2005 NDAA made this increase permanent. Most recently, the House-passed version of the FY2011 NDAA[17] provided for a $35 per month increase in Hostile Fire/Imminent Danger Pay.

This increase was not supported by the Senate and was not included in the enacted version of the NDAA.

Hardship Duty Pay

Military personnel serving in Iraq, Afghanistan, parts of the Persian Gulf region, and certain nearby areas are also eligible for Hardship Duty Pay (HDP), authorized by 37 USC. 305. It is compensation for the exceptional demands of certain duty, including unusually demanding mission assignments (HDP-Mission), locations with extreme climates or austere facilities (HDP-Location), or for an involuntary extension of duty (HDP-Involuntary Extension).[18]

The maximum amount of HDP previously permitted by the statute was $300 per month; this maximum was increased to $750 per month by the FY2006 NDAA and then raised to $1,500 per month by the FY2008 NDAA. While these increases have been significant, the actual DOD-approved rate for HDP for both Iraq and Afghanistan is, and has been, $100 per month.

Family Separation Allowance

Military personnel participating in OEF and OIF/OND may also be eligible for Family Separation Allowance (FSA). FSA is authorized by 37 USC. 427, which provides a special pay for those servicemembers *with dependents* who are separated from their families for more than 30 days. The purpose of this pay is to "partially reimburse, on average, members of the uniformed services involuntarily separated from their dependents for the reasonable amount of extra expenses that result from such separation...." To be eligible for this allowance, US military personnel must be separated from their dependents for 30 continuous days or more; but once the 30-day threshold has been reached, the allowance is applied retroactively to the first day of separation.

The authorizing statute for FSA sets the rate at $250 per month. The House-passed version of the FY2011 NDAA[19] also recommended increasing FSA by $35 a month to $285.

Again, this legislation was not supported by the Senate and was not included in the enacted version of the NDAA.[20]

Per Diem

Military personnel serving in OIF/OND/OEF are also entitled to per diem payments of $105 per month; the rate is the same for all personnel.

Savings Deposit Program

Another benefit available to those deployed to Afghanistan, Iraq, and other designated areas nearby is eligibility for the Savings Deposit Program. This program allows service members to earn a guaranteed rate of 10% interest on deposits of up to $10,000, which must have been earned in the designated areas. The deposit is normally returned to the servicemember, with interest, within 90 days after he or she leaves the eligible region, although earlier withdrawals can sometimes be made for emergency reasons.

Combat Zone Tax Exclusion

One of the more generous benefits for many of those serving overseas in OEF or OIF is the "combat zone tax exclusion." Certain areas in the Persian Gulf region—including Iraq and the airspace above it—have been designated combat zones since the 1990-1991 Persian Gulf War. Afghanistan and the airspace above it have been designated a "combat zone" since September 19, 2001. Military personnel serving in direct support of operations in these combat zones are also eligible for the combat zone tax exclusion. For enlisted personnel and warrant officers, this means that all compensation for active military service in a combat zone is free of federal income tax. For commissioned officers, their compensation is free of federal income tax up to the maximum amount of enlisted basic pay plus any imminent danger pay received. While this benefit applies only to federal income tax, almost all states have provisions extending the benefit to their state income tax as well.

In addition, military personnel who receive a reenlistment bonus while stationed in a combat zone do not have to pay federal income tax on any of the bonus. The amounts involved can be substantial. For example, the Army recently increased reenlistment bonuses for Special Forces NCOs to a lump sum of $150,000 for a six-year reenlistment; $75,000 for five years; $50,000 for four years; and $30,000, $18,000, and $8,000 for three years, two years, and one year respectively. The 2006 NDAA boosted the maximum reenlistment bonus for career soldiers other than Special Forces to $90,000.[21]

Rest and Recreation (R&R) for Personnel in OIF/OND/OEF

As has been widely reported, military personnel serving 12-month tours of duty in Iraq and Afghanistan are entitled to one 15-day period of "R&R" or home leave in the United States during their tour. Initially the program was designed to fund the travel of personnel from either theater of operations to several major "gateway" airports in the United States and any further travel within the United States had to be funded by the individual. However, Congress has since authorized funding of internal travel within the United States. Reimbursement will be for the military member's travel; there is no funding for dependent travel to meet military personnel on R&R. (There has been some funding of such dependent travel by private charitable organizations.)

8. What Cash Lump-Sum Death Benefits Are Available to the Survivors of Military Personnel Killed in Iraq or Afghanistan?

Currently, the survivors (usually spouses or parents) of military personnel who die while serving in Operations Iraqi Freedom, New Dawn, or Enduring Freedom (OIF, OND or OEF) are entitled to several lump-sum monetary benefits. These include a $100,000 death gratuity, payable within a few days of the death to assist families in dealing with immediate expenses; a $255 Social Security lump sum; coverage of burial expenses up to $6,900 [a Department of Veterans Affairs (VA) benefit]; and Servicemembers' Group Life Insurance (SGLI)[22] of $400,000.[23] There are also a wide range of recurring-payment survivor benefits from both DOD and the VA, as well as non-monetary benefits.[24]

For more information on military death benefits, see CRS Report RL31334, *Operations Noble Eagle, Enduring Freedom, and Iraqi Freedom: Questions and Answers About US Military Personnel, Compensation, and Force Structure*, by Lawrence Kapp and Charles A. Henning; and CRS Report RL32783, *FY2005 Supplemental Appropriations for Iraq and Afghanistan, Tsunami Relief, and Other Activities*, by Amy Belasco and Larry Nowels.

End Notes

[1] Basic pay is monthly compensation that all military personnel in the same pay grade and with the same number of years of service will receive.

[2] As defined by Section 101 of Title 10 USC., the term "grade" refers to a step or degree within a military rank while "rank" means an order of precedence among members of the armed forces. Commissioned officers have been assigned pay grades 0-1 through 0-10, warrant

officers have been assigned W-1 through W-5 and enlisted personnel have been designated as E-1 through E-9.

[3] Some pay grades, especially those of lower ranking personnel, are "capped" at designated oints, generally because they should have been promoted to the next higher grade. For example, the last longevity increase for E-5 (Sergeant in the Army and Marine Corps, Staff Sergeant in the Air Force and Petty Officer Second Class in the Navy) occurs at "Over 12" while the final increase of 0-5 (Lieutenant Colonel in the Army, Air Force and Marine Corps) occurs at "Over 22."

[4] Military Compensation Background Papers: Compensation Elements and Related Manpower Cost Items, Their Purposes and Legislative Backgrounds, Sixth Edition, April 2005.

[5] Section 601, P.L. 109-364.

[6] Section 601, P.L. 109-364.

[7] Section 642, P.L. 109-364.

[8] For a detailed discussion of the costs and value of monetary and non-monetary benefits, see Military Compensation: Balancing Cash and Noncash Benefits, Economic and Budget Issue Brief, Congressional Budget Office, January 16, 2004.

[9] Maze, Rick, "DoD seeks targeted raises of up to 8.3 percent," Army Times, March 20, 2005.

[10] "Evaluating Military Compensation", Congressional Budget Office, June, 2007, p.2.

[11] "Pay Raise: 1.4% Assured; 1,9% Unlikely", Tom Philpott, December 9, 2010.

[12] See, for example, Office of the Under Secretary of Defense for Personnel and Readiness. Report of the Ninth Quadrennial Review of Military Compensation. Vol. I. Washington, March 2002: passim, but especially 29-74, 137-82, 188-89; and Asch, Beth J., and James R. Hosek. "Military Compensation: Trends and Policy Options," Documented Briefing. Santa Monica, CA, RAND Corporation, 1999.

[13] US General Accounting Office [now Government Accountability Office], Military Personnel: Active Duty Benefits Reflect Changing Demographics, but Opportunities Exist to Improve, GAO-02-935, September 18, 2002.

[14] The Quadrennial Review of Military Compensation or QRMC is required every four years by 37 USC. 1008(b). The 10th QRMC was convened in August 2005 and submitted the final portion of its report in July 2008. Volume 1, which included the recommendations concerning the pay gap, can be viewed at http://www.defenselink/mil/prhome/docs/Tenth_QRMC_feb2008_Vol%20I.pdf.

[15] Operation Iraqi Freedom became Operation New Dawn (OND) on September 1, 2010.

[16] Much of this material is taken from CRS Report RL31334, Operations Noble Eagle, Enduring Freedom, and Iraqi Freedom: Questions and Answers About US Military Personnel, Compensation, and Force Structure, by Lawrence Kapp and Charles A. Henning.

[17] Section 618, H.Rept. 111-491, May 21, 2010.

[18] To support the surge in Iraq, a number of units were involuntarily extended from the original 12-month deployment to a revised 15-month deployment. Soldiers assigned to these units were authorized an additional $200/month HDP during this 3-month extension.

[19] Section 604, H.Rept. 111-491, May 21, 2010.

[21] Section 629, National Defense Authorization Act for Fiscal Year 2006, December 18, 2005.

[22] All servicemembers are automatically enrolled in this benefit, which is paid for by an approximate $16 monthly deduction from pay, members may opt out or reduce coverage, but less than 1% do so.

[23] The death gratuity and the SGLI maximum amount were raised substantially by the FY2005 Supplemental Appropriations Act for Defense, the Global War on Terror, and Tsunami Relief (the "FY2005 Supplemental") (P.L. 109-13, May 11, 2005; 119 Stat. 231). The death gratuity was raised from $12,420 to $100,000; and the maximum SGLI coverage was raised

from $250,000 to $400,000 with the first $150,000 provided free for personnel in a combat zone. Because these increases are in an FY2005 appropriation law, they were scheduled to expire at the end of FY2005. However, the 2006 NDAA applied the $100,000 death gratuity to all active-duty deaths (not just those that were combat-related) and made the payments retroactive to October 7, 2001. In addition, survivors of service members who died of non-combat causes on active duty between October 7, 2001, and the date of enactment of the 2006 NDAA received retroactive payments of $150,000. This latter payment closed an SGLI loophole. The FY2007 John Warner National Defense Authorization Act increased the amount of "free" SGLI coverage from $150,000 to $400,000 for all servicemembers serving in OIF and OEF.

[24] For the earlier legislative history of some of these benefits, monetary and non-monetary, see Office of the Secretary of Defense. Military Compensation Background Papers. Sixth Edition. April 2005. A more detailed summary of all such benefits and a comparison of them with federal civilian and state and local government survivor benefits is at US Government Accountability Office, Military Personnel: Survivor Benefits for Servicemembers and Federal, State, and City Government Employees, GAO-04-814, July 2004.

In: Military Pay and Benefits
Editor: Walter Avraham

Chapter 3

MILITARY CASH INCENTIVES: DOD SHOULD COORDINATE AND MONITOR ITS EFFORTS TO ACHIEVE COST-EFFECTIVE BONUSES AND SPECIAL PAYS[*]

United States Government Accountability Office

ABBREVIATIONS

AFQT	Armed Forces Qualification Test
AAF	Army Advantage Fund
ACIP	Aviation Career Incentive Pay
ACP	Aviation Continuation Pay
DOD	Department of Defense
OSD	Office of the Secretary of Defense
SRB	Selective Reenlistment Bonus

---

[*] This is an edited, reformatted and augmented version of The United States Government Accountability Office publication, Report to Congressional Committees, GAO-11-631, dated June 2011.

June 21, 2011

Congressional Committees

The Department of Defense (DOD) spent about $5.6 billion in fiscal year 2010 on special and incentive pays and bonuses for active-duty servicemembers.[1] Of that amount, about $1.2 billion was contracted for enlistment and reenlistment bonuses. DOD uses these incentives and bonuses as tools in its compensation system to help ensure that military pay is sufficient to field a high-quality, all-volunteer force, including those in hard-to-fill or critical specialties. Special pays and bonuses comprise about 5 percent of DOD's budget for cash compensation and less than 1 percent of its overall budget. In addition to cash compensation, which includes bonuses and basic pay, the department provides active-duty personnel with a comprehensive compensation package that includes noncash benefits, such as health care, and deferred compensation, such as retirement pensions.[2]

In 2005, we recommended that DOD assess its compensation system's effectiveness, including an analysis of the reasonableness and appropriateness of its allocation of cash and benefits.[3] DOD agreed with our recommendation, stating that it was already engaged in multiple efforts to assess its compensation strategy. Subsequently, the Senate report to accompany a bill for the National Defense Authorization Act for Fiscal Year 2011 (S. 3454)[4] directed GAO to assess DOD's and the services' use of cash incentives to recruit and retain highly qualified individuals for service in the armed forces to fill hard-to-fill or critical wartime specialties and review the extent to which the services have an effective process for designating an occupation as critical or hard-to-fill. Effective management of cash incentives is particularly important, given the current budgetary environment and the Secretary of Defense's initiatives to instill a culture of savings and cost accountability across DOD.[5] Moreover, the Secretary of Defense has acknowledged and expressed concern about growing personnel costs crowding out DOD's ability to spend on its other needs. Accordingly, this report (1) identifies recent trends in the services' use of enlistment and reenlistment bonuses, (2) assesses the extent to which the services have processes that enable them to determine which occupational specialties should be offered bonuses and whether bonus amounts are optimally set, and (3) determines how much flexibility DOD has in managing selected special and incentive pays for officer and enlisted personnel.

To determine the recent trends in the use of enlistment and reenlistment bonuses, we analyzed service data on contracted enlistment and reenlistment bonuses for fiscal years 2006 through 2010. To evaluate the extent to which the services have processes to designate occupations that should be offered bonuses and whether bonus amounts are optimally set, we reviewed DOD and service regulations pertaining to their processes for designating bonus-eligible occupations. We also interviewed relevant DOD and service officials with responsibilities for designating occupations as bonus eligible and obtained information on analytical tools such as statistical models used by the services to identify bonus-eligible occupations. To determine how much flexibility DOD has in managing selected special and incentive pays, we analyzed data on 15 special and incentive pays across the services for fiscal years 2006 through 2010, which represented the top five expenditures for special and incentive pays each year for each service. We focused on pays that were available to most servicemembers. For this reason, we excluded medical pays. We conducted this performance audit from September 2010 through June 2011 in accordance with generally accepted government auditing standards. These standards require that we plan and perform the audit to obtain sufficient, appropriate evidence to provide a reasonable basis for our findings and conclusions based on our research objectives. We believe that the evidence obtained provides a reasonable basis for our findings and conclusions based on our audit objectives. (See app. I for further details on our scope and methodology.)

BACKGROUND

DOD is one of the nation's largest employers, with more than 1.4 million active-duty personnel (as of March 2011). To fulfill its mission of maintaining national security, DOD must meet its human capital needs by recruiting, retaining, and motivating a large number of qualified individuals, though the requirement for new recruits has declined in the last couple of years (see table 1 for the numbers of accessions and reenlistments from fiscal years 2006 through 2010). The Office of the Secretary of Defense for Personnel and Readiness is principally responsible for establishing active-duty compensation policy.

In 1962, the Gorham Commission adopted the term "regular military compensation" to be used to compare military and civilian-sector pay. Regular military compensation is defined as the sum of basic pay, allowances for housing and subsistence, and federal tax advantage. In addition to regular military compensation, DOD also uses over 60 authorized special and incentive pays, including various enlistment and selective reenlistment bonuses, to offer incentives to undertake or continue service in a particular specialty or type of duty assignment. According to DOD, special pays are used to selectively address specific force management needs, such as staffing shortfalls in particular occupational areas, hazardous or otherwise less desirable duty assignments, and attainment and retention of valuable skills. In addition, in certain occupational categories, such as technical and professional fields, special pays are used to help ensure pay comparability with civilian sector salaries. OSD believes that these pays offer flexibility to the compensation system not otherwise available through the basic pay table.[6]

Table 1. Number of Accessions and Reenlistments by Service for Fiscal Years 2006-2010

			Accessions		
Fiscal Year	Army	Navy	Marine Corps	Air Force	Total
2006	80,635	36,679	32,337	30,889	180,540
2007	80,407	37,361	35,603	27,800	181,171
2008	80,517	38,485	37,991	27,848	184,841
2009	70,044	35,519	31,407	31,983	168,953
2010	74,577	34,180	28,040	28,637	165,434
			Reenlistments		
Fiscal Year	Army	Navy	Marine Corps	Air Force	Total
2006	67,307	25,970	13,255	36,235	142,767
2007	69,777	25,539	17,695	35,073	148,084
2008	73,913	26,510	16,696	20,650	137,769
2009	68,387	30,895	16,001	35,598	150,881
2010	68,105	35,525	14,265	35,501	153,396

Source: DOD.

To provide guidance to the services on managing their enlistment and reenlistment bonus programs, the Office of the Secretary of Defense (OSD) issued DOD Directive 1304.21.[7] Under this directive, the Principal Deputy Under Secretary of Defense for Personnel and Readiness is assigned responsibilities including monitoring certain bonus programs carried out by the services. Specifically, the Principal Deputy Under Secretary of Defense for Personnel and Readiness is responsible for establishing (1) criteria for designating military specialties that qualify for these bonuses, (2) criteria for individual members' eligibility for these bonuses, and (3) reporting and data requirements for the periodic review and evaluation of these bonus programs. The Principal Deputy Under Secretary of Defense for Personnel and Readiness is also responsible for recommending to the Secretary of Defense measures required to attain the most efficient use of resources devoted to these programs.

As required by 37 U.S.C. § 1008, at least once every 4 years, the President directs a review of the principles and concepts of the military compensation system. These regular studies are called the Quadrennial Reviews of Military Compensation and typically focus on issues such as achieving flexibility and promoting fairness in compensation. The most recent Quadrennial Review was completed in 2008 and offered a number of recommendations, including simplifying the structure of special and incentive pays.

We have completed a body of work on military compensation and enlistment and reenlistment bonuses. For example, in April 2010, we reported on the comparison of military to civilian pay.[8] In a 2009 report, we evaluated the Army's use of bonuses and determined that the Army did not know whether it was paying more than it needed to pay to get a cost-effective return on investment.[9] In that report, we recommended that the Army build on available analyses to set cost-effective enlistment and reenlistment bonuses in order to avoid making excessive payments. As a result of our report, the Army significantly reduced its enlistment and reenlistment bonus program; however, the reductions were not based on specific analysis that determined the cost-effective bonus amount.

DOD's Contracted Bonus Amounts Were 58 Percent Less in 2010 than in 2008, Its Peak Year

DOD contracted $1.2 billion in fiscal year 2010 for enlistment and reenlistment bonuses, an amount that was 58 percent less than the $2.8 billion contracted in fiscal year 2008, its peak year.[10] For the services, total contracted bonus amounts peaked in fiscal years 2008 or 2009 and then decreased. (See fig. 1.) Specifically, for fiscal years 2006 through 2009, total contracted amounts for bonuses rose for the Air Force and the Marine Corps and declined thereafter by 16 percent and 64 percent, respectively. For the Army and the Navy, contracted amounts increased through fiscal year 2008 and then declined by 78 percent and 40 percent, respectively. Though the Air Force contracted the least of all the services for bonuses from fiscal years 2006 to 2009, the total contracted amount increased by 254 percent during that period, from $100 million to $352 million. The Air Force attributes this increase, in part, to the reenlistment bonus program being underfunded in fiscal year 2006. In addition, the Air Force believes that the increase was necessary to ensure that its hard-tofill occupational specialties, such as battlefield airmen, were filled and to accommodate the high operations tempo necessary for the war in Iraq and Afghanistan. During the same time, the Marine Corps increased the amounts contracted by 398 percent, from $108 million to $540 million. The Marine Corps attributes this increase to the 2007 presidential Grow-theForce initiative, which required the Marine Corps to increase its number of active-duty personnel by 27,000. The Army also increased as part of the Grow-the-Force initiative; its total contracted amounts increased by 15 percent from fiscal years 2006 to 2008. When growing the force, the Army stated that it was not targeting bonuses to hard-to-fill or critical specialties but rather was focused on meeting its overall recruiting mission. As a result, once the Army met 99 percent of its growth in fiscal year 2008, it began to pay fewer bonuses and target them to personnel with specific critical skill sets, such as divers and satellite communication systems operators/maintainers. Between fiscal years 2006 to 2008, the Navy increased its total bonus funds by 13 percent. Navy officials attribute this increase, in part, to the low unemployment rates for years 2007 and 2008 and the need to provide incentives to retain sailors with more options for postmilitary employment.

From fiscal years 2006 through 2010, DOD contracted $11 billion for enlistment and reenlistment bonuses (in constant fiscal year 2010 dollars). Of this total, the Army accounted for approximately half, and the Air Force for the least amount, at 9 percent (see fig. 2). During this time, DOD reported that the active components of all four services met or exceeded their numeric goals for enlisted accessions and, with the exception of the Army in fiscal years 2006 through 2008, the active components of the services also met their benchmarks for recruit quality.[11] For retention, the services generally met their goals but not in all years.[12]

With the exception of the Army, the services contracted more on their reenlistment bonus programs than on their enlistment bonus programs. Of the $11 billion in contracted bonuses by all the services, $4.5 billion, or 40 percent, was for enlistment bonuses, and $6.6 billion, or 60 percent, was for reenlistment bonuses.

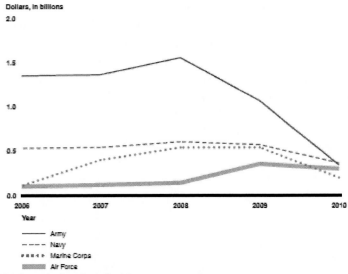

Source: GAO analysis of service data.

Figure 1. Trends in Bonuses Contracted by Service, Fiscal Years 2006 through 2010, in Constant Fiscal Year 2010 Dollars.

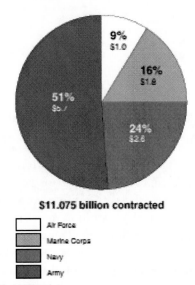

Source: GAO analysis of service data.

Figure 2. Percentage of $11 Billion Contracted for Enlistment and Selective Reenlistment Bonuses by Each Military Service, Fiscal Years 2006 through 2010.

Army officials said they were paying high enlistment bonuses to achieve very high accession rates beginning in 2005 because of the negative publicity surrounding the wars in Iraq and Afghanistan, coupled with a strong economy and high employment rates from 2005 to 2008. In addition, the Army was to increase its end strength, consistent with the "Grow-the-Force" plan, from approximately 480,000 to approximately 547,000. To meet this goal, the Army also had to retain greater numbers of personnel.

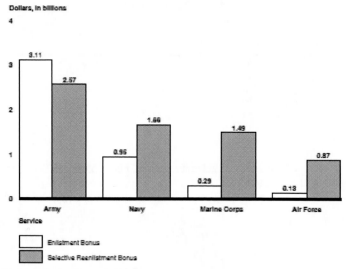

Source: GAO analysis of service data.

Figure 3. Total Amounts Contracted by Each Service for Enlistment and Reenlistment Bonuses, Fiscal Years 2006 through 2010, in Constant Fiscal Year 2010 Dollars.

Unlike the Army, the Navy, Air Force, and Marine Corps contracted a greater portion of their overall bonus amounts on reenlistment, rather than enlistment, bonuses (see fig. 3). According to the Navy, more is spent on reenlistment bonuses because the cost to replace trained sailors is significant due to long training programs, high attrition rates, and a high demand for the occupations they are trained for in the civilian sector such as those trained in nuclear occupations. Similarly, the Air Force attributed its greater spending on reenlistment bonuses to the competition with the private sector for trained and experienced airmen.

The Air Force also stated that the eligible population for reenlistment bonuses is much larger than for enlistment bonuses and the Air Force has a training investment in these experienced servicemembers.

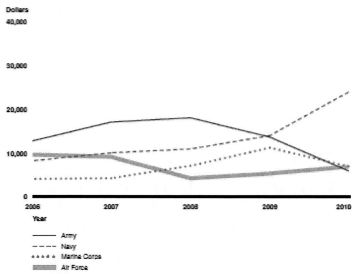

Source: GAO analysis of service data.

Figure 4. Average Amounts of Enlistment Bonuses, Fiscal Years 2006 through 2010, in Constant Fiscal Year 2010 Dollars.

According to the Marine Corps, its focus has also been on retaining proven combat leaders, and it has therefore been targeting the majority of its discretionary funding[13] on retention rather than accessions. In addition, the Marine Corps stated that the Marine Corps "sells itself" to potential applicants and therefore needs to offer enlistment bonuses only for certain hard-to-fill occupations.

The services also varied in the average amounts of bonuses. From fiscal years 2006 through 2008, the Army's average per-person enlistment bonuses were higher than those of the other services (see fig. 4).

For example, in fiscal year 2008, the Army's average enlistment bonus was $18,085, while the Air Force's was only $4,271. However, in fiscal years 2009 and 2010, the Navy's average per-person enlistment bonus amounts were higher than those of all the other services. For example, in fiscal year 2010, the Navy's average enlistment bonus was $23,957, while the Army's was $5,969. Navy officials stated that, during this period, it began to give bonuses to fewer personnel, but those personnel were given higher bonuses, thus driving the average up.

With respect to reenlistment bonuses, the Air Force's average per-person bonus amount was higher than those of the other services from fiscal years 2006 through 2008.

The Army's average per-person bonus amount was smaller than those of the other services from fiscal years 2006 through 2010, ranging from $13,796 to $4,392 (see fig. 5).

In contrast, for fiscal years 2006 through 2008, the Air Force's average per-person reenlistment bonus amounts were higher than the other services', ranging from $32,667 to $36,247. The Marine Corps' average was highest of all the services' in fiscal year 2009, at $36,753; and the Navy's average was highest in fiscal year 2010, at $32,719. According to Navy officials, the Navy needs to retain highly skilled sailors who have undergone extensive training for skills that are marketable in private industry and require arduous missions. For example, officials commented that the SEALs are the first in line when infiltrating military targets in dangerous environments, and their skills have been sought by private contractors; as a result, their bonuses tend to be higher.

Navy officials also said that the length and cost of training nuclear personnel makes the opportunity cost for retraining a new sailor greater than the bonus.

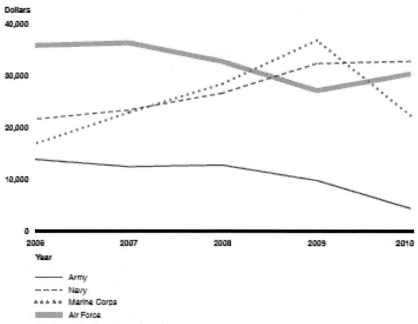

Source: GAO analysis of service data.

Figure 5. Average Amounts of Selective Reenlistment Bonuses, Fiscal Years 2006 through 2010, in Constant Fiscal Year 2010 Dollars.

THE SERVICES HAVE PROCESSES FOR IDENTIFYING OCCUPATIONS THAT ARE HARD TO FILL BUT NOT FOR IDENTIFYING THE MOST COST-EFFECTIVE BONUS AMOUNTS

The services have processes in place that include the analysis of data on how difficult it is to retain and recruit particular occupations and the subjective judgment of personnel who are involved in managing these occupations. DOD guidance allows the military departments the flexibility to offer a bonus to any occupation that meets certain criteria, such as being hard to fill or retain, and they may adjust bonuses as market conditions change. However, although much research has been conducted on bonuses' effects on enlistment and retention, DOD does not know whether the services have been paying more than necessary to meet their recruiting and retention goals. Identifying optimal bonus amounts is challenging because such studies must control for the numerous, changing factors that affect individuals' recruiting and retention decisions, such as the unemployment rate, the deployment rate resulting from overseas operations, and the changing public perceptions of the war.

The Services Have Processes for Determining Bonus-Eligible Occupations

The services' processes for determining which occupations should be offered enlistment or reenlistment bonuses include the use of models.[14] While the services use different models, they generally incorporate factors such as data on occupations that have historically received bonuses, attrition and retention rates for these occupations, and the current population for each occupation. Models for determining eligibility for enlistment bonuses include data on occupational fill rates and available training slots for particular occupations. Models for determining reenlistment bonuses include data on the retention rates of and projected future shortages in particular occupations.

In addition to using models, the services seek stakeholder input on their bonus program plans. Stakeholders include personnel managers who have experience with the occupations being discussed and can contribute information that cannot be provided by the models, such as whether servicemembers in a particular occupation are experiencing unusual difficulties. Stakeholder input is provided differently across the services but is consistently used to make adjustments to data provided by the models. For example, the Army and the Navy consider stakeholder input through formal meetings. Specifically, the Army formally holds Enlisted Incentives Review Boards each quarter that include personnel from the Army Recruiting Command and the Army Human Resources Command. During these board meetings, stakeholders discuss which occupations should receive a bonus, whether these bonuses are appropriately set, and come to a consensus on how much each bonus should be during the next quarter. The Navy, in addition to a monthly review of the bonus program, formally convenes a working group three to four times per year for reenlistment bonuses where personnel managers responsible for monitoring and managing the retention health of occupations present opinions and analysis as to whether the recommendations for bonus amounts are set appropriately or need adjustments. In contrast, the Marine Corps and Air Force utilize a less formal approach to stakeholder input. For example, to obtain input on their projected enlistment bonus award plans, Marine Corps and Air Force bonus program managers seek input from their recruiting and human resources personnel, who provide their perspectives on projected future shortages. As part of the process, all services stressed that regardless of whether bonus levels are produced by models or stakeholder input, in the end, bonus amounts must be adjusted to fit into the services' fiscal budgets.

OSD guidance allows the military departments flexibility to offer bonuses to occupations that they are having difficulty filling. OSD guidance to the services on administering their bonus programs states that the intent of bonuses is to influence personnel inventories in situations in which less costly methods have proven inadequate or impractical.[15] The guidance also states that the military skills selected for the award of bonuses must be essential to the accomplishment of defense missions. Additionally, the guidance sets forth some general criteria to use when identifying bonus-eligible occupations. For enlistment bonuses, the Secretaries of the military departments are to consider, among other things, the attainment of total accession objectives, priority of the skill, year group and pay grade shortages, and length and cost of training. For reenlistment bonuses, the Secretaries of the military department concerned are to consider, among other things, critical personnel shortages, retention in relation to objectives, high training cost, and arduousness or unattractiveness of the occupation. These general criteria provided by OSD allow each Secretary of a military department to determine what occupations should be considered essential and therefore eligible for bonuses. Because the criteria OSD lists in its guidance are broadly defined and because the Secretaries of the military departments are purposely given the flexibility to adjust which occupations they believe need to be offered bonuses as conditions change, the departments are given the authority to award bonuses to any occupation under certain conditions. That is, all service occupations could be considered essential to the accomplishment of defense missions if the department is experiencing difficulty filling them. Service officials told us that this flexibility allows the departments to adjust bonuses quickly as market conditions change. An Army official explained that, for example, in some cases an occupation such as cook may need a bonus because personnel do not want to be assigned to it.

The Services Monitor the Performance of Their Bonus Programs but Lack Information on the Most Cost-Effective Bonus Amounts

All services regularly monitor the performance of their enlistment and reenlistment bonus programs. With respect to measuring the performance of their enlistment bonus programs, all services said that they continuously monitor their progress in meeting recruiting goals. For example, Army officials told us that they use the quarterly recruiting numbers within each occupational specialty as indicators of the effectiveness of the Army's enlistment bonus program. If they notice that an occupation is lagging behind or that recruiters have been particularly successful in meeting goals for an occupation, the quarterly Enlisted Incentives Review Board provides an opportunity for the Army to move that occupation to a level associated with a higher or lower bonus amount.[16] The Army then continues to monitor its recruiting numbers to gauge whether this change has worked. With respect to measuring the performance of the retention bonus programs, all services monitor their progress in meeting their retention goals. For example, Navy officials said they review the percentage of reenlistment goals achieved for each occupational specialty and use that information to increase or decrease bonus amounts.

With both enlistment and reenlistment bonuses, the services take a certain amount of risk when changing bonus amounts, but officials told us that continuous monitoring of the recruiting and retention data allows them to make necessary adjustments. Moreover, officials also told us that they are not willing to take too much of a risk with some critical occupations. For example, Navy officials said that, given the length and cost of training nuclear personnel, the high qualifications that these personnel must have, and the high marketability of their skills in the private sector, the Navy sees bonuses for these occupations as essential. The services have been relying on the analyses of recruiting and retention data to determine whether their bonus programs have produced intended results, but these data alone are not sufficient to help ensure that bonus levels are set at the most cost-effective amounts. Just as for any government program, resources available for bonuses are finite, and increasing bonuses for some groups or occupations must come at the expense of incentives for other groups or occupations. Service officials agreed that their existing approach of monitoring the performance of bonus programs by looking at recruiting and retention data does not tell them what specific bonus amounts are most cost-effective and whether their goals could be achieved with a smaller bonus amount or a different, and possibly less costly, combination of incentives.

OSD guidance indicates that officials must exercise bonus authorities in a cost-effective manner. According to DOD Directive 1304.21 and DOD Instruction 1304.29,[17] bonuses are intended for specific situations in which less costly methods have proven inadequate or impractical. DOD Directive 1304.21 also states that it is wasteful to use financial incentives when less costly but equally effective actions are available. Further, in its 2006 report, the Defense Advisory Committee on Military Compensation set forth principles for guiding the military compensation system, one of which called on the military compensation system to meet force management objectives in the least costly manner.[18]

There is an extensive body of research on bonus effectiveness, but much of it does not assess the cost-effectiveness of specific bonus amounts. Over the years, the services and other organizations have conducted extensive research on the use of cash incentives, some of it dating back to the 1960s and 1970s. This research has generally shown that bonuses have a positive effect on the recruitment and retention of military personnel, even after controlling for a variety of demographic, economic, and other factors. Additionally, a study issued by RAND in 1986 specifically considered the cost-effectiveness of bonuses. RAND analyzed the results of a nationwide experiment to assess the effects of varying enlistment bonus amounts, showing that cash bonuses were extremely effective at channeling high-quality individuals into the traditionally hard-to-fill occupations. Furthermore, RAND found that increased bonuses had the effect of both bringing more people into the service and lengthening the terms of their commitment.[19] However, according to DOD and the researchers interviewed, there is no recent work focused on the cost-effectiveness of specific bonus amounts.[20]

We cited some of this research in a 1988 report on the advantages and disadvantages of a draft versus an all-volunteer force[21] and, more recently, in a 2009 report on the Army's use of incentives to increase its end strength.[22] In the 2009 report, which focused on the Army, we determined that the Army did not know whether it was paying more than it needed to pay to get a cost-effective return on investment, and we recommended that the Army build on available analyses to set cost-effective enlistment and reenlistment bonuses in order to avoid making excessive payments. DOD concurred with our recommendation and commissioned RAND to conduct a study to implement it. The study, released in June 2010, found that bonuses were an important and flexible tool in meeting recruiting and retention objectives, particularly for the Army, but did not assess whether bonuses were set too high. [23] According to DOD, a detailed study for bonus amounts was beyond the scope of the RAND study. DOD wanted that study to determine whether bonuses in general were an efficient and effective use of resources for recruiting and retention and how these bonuses compared with other incentives. DOD believes that determining what bonus amounts are optimal is significant and complex enough to warrant its own study and plans to pursue that line of effort when sufficient resources are available. At present, however, it has no immediate plans to do so.

We recognize that identifying optimal bonus amounts is challenging because such studies must control for the numerous, changing factors that affect individuals' recruiting and retention decisions, such as the unemployment rate, the deployment rate resulting from overseas operations, and the changing public perceptions of the war. Despite these challenges, research organizations and some of the services have been considering various approaches that could be used for that purpose. Several research organizations have developed specific methodologies for conducting studies on the cost-effectiveness of bonuses.[24] For example, one research organization submitted a proposal to DOD and the Army to develop an econometric model[25] for determining the most cost-effective bonus amounts for different occupations. Another research organization is considering the use of an experiment,[26] in combination with an econometric model, for determining the minimal amounts of bonuses needed to fill different occupations and had informally shared its ideas with DOD. The researchers interviewed considered the costs of such research to be modest and expected the benefits of any potential improvements to the services' bonus programs resulting from such research to outweigh the costs, particularly given the billions of dollars that the services have spent on bonuses over the years.

According to DOD, service officials are interested in this type of research, which would provide them with information needed to more effectively manage limited resources in their bonus programs. In fact, some services have already taken steps toward obtaining this information. For example, the Army has funded an econometric model developed by a research organization to predict the likelihood of applicants' choosing particular occupational specialties as a function of various factors, including bonuses offered. According to an Army official, this model would allow the Army to evaluate alternative cash incentive packages needed to fill specific occupations, thus optimizing its recruiting resources. The Navy uses an econometric model developed 10 years ago by a research organization, which Navy officials told us allows them to predict the extent to which a mix of recruiting resources, including varying bonus amounts, would enable them to meet recruiting goals. Although Navy officials said that this model does not provide information on recruiting outcomes within specific occupations, it helps them determine which bonus amounts would be needed to meet the overall recruiting mission.

While efforts to develop ways to assess the cost-effectiveness of bonuses have been made by some research organizations and have generated interest at the individual service level, OSD has not coordinated research in this area. The Principal Deputy Under Secretary of Defense for Personnel and Readiness is responsible for monitoring the bonus programs of the military services and recommending to the Secretary of Defense measures required to attain the most efficient use of resources devoted to the programs. The Office of the Under Secretary of Defense for Personnel and Readiness therefore has a role in monitoring individual service efforts to assess the cost-effectiveness of bonuses, which could be facilitated by information-sharing among the services on this issue. OSD recognizes the importance of having information on the cost-effectiveness of bonuses and using that information to guide the services' management of their bonus programs. OSD officials stated that they are in constant contact with the services regarding their use of bonuses and facilitate conferences, working groups, and other meetings that allow the services to discuss their incentive programs. Moreover, the development of statistical models for assessing bonus effectiveness is one of the fiscal year 2012 research priorities for the Accessions Policy office within the Office of the Under Secretary of Defense for Personnel and Readiness.

However, to date, OSD has not facilitated the exchange of information among the services on how best to conduct research on the cost-effectiveness of bonuses, what efficiencies could be gained from such efforts, and whether to jointly undertake them. Without such information-sharing, the services may not be able to fully take advantage of existing and emerging methodologies for assessing cost-effectiveness, share lessons learned, and ultimately obtain critical information needed to know whether they are getting the best return on their bonus investments.

DOD IS IN THE PROCESS OF INCREASING ITS FLEXIBILITY IN MANAGING SPECIAL AND INCENTIVE PAYS BUT LACKS BASELINE MEASURES TO ASSESS OUTCOMES

DOD has begun to increase its flexibility in managing special and incentive pays, as authorized by the National Defense Authorization Act for Fiscal Year 2008.[27] According to DOD, special and incentive pays are intended to provide the services with flexible compensation dollars that can be used to address specific staffing needs and other force management issues that cannot be efficiently addressed through basic pay increases. However, while DOD has discretionary authority to determine the amount and the recipients of enlistment and reenlistment bonuses based on personnel needs, it did not previously have similar discretion to adjust pays where the amounts and eligibility criteria are specified by law. According to DOD, a significant number of special and incentive pays paid to military personnel have been statutorily prescribed. In our review of 15 special and incentive pays, 6 are currently entitlement pays and accounted for $3.9 billion, or 29 percent, of the $13.6 billion expended on the 15 special and incentive pays from fiscal years 2006 through 2010.[28] Of the 15 pays we reviewed, DOD has not yet exercised its authority to consolidate all of them and thereby increase its flexibility in managing who receives these pays and how much recipients are paid. Specifically, DOD has not yet consolidated pays in the following categories: Aviation Career Incentive Pay; Career Sea Pay; Submarine Duty Incentive Pay; Hazardous Duty Incentive Pay, which includes Crew Member Flying Duty Pay; and Parachute Duty Pay.

The differences in flexibility DOD has in managing entitlement pays that are currently required by statute compared with discretionary pays are illustrated by the two special and incentive pays that the services give to aviation officers: Aviation Career Incentive Pay (ACIP) and Aviation Continuation Pay (ACP). The services have specific statutory guidelines that require certain levels of payment and define the personnel who receive ACIP until this pay is consolidated with other flight pays. If a servicemember meets the aviation criteria outlined in 37 U.S.C. § 301a, he or she is entitled to this special pay on a graded scale that depends on years of flying experience. The payments range from $125 to $840 a month. Officer aviators who meet the statutory criteria are entitled by law to this monthly supplement regardless of individual assignments.[29] In other words, payment does not vary according to type of aircraft, training required, or any other measure services might use to differentiate aviator assignments. By comparison, ACP is a special pay authority that is used as a retention bonus for officers who have completed their active-duty service obligations to incentivize them to remain on active duty. Unlike the restrictions currently applicable to administering ACIP, DOD and the services have the discretion to decide who should get ACP and how much to pay—up to the statutory maximum of $25,000 per year.

The flexibility the services currently have in administering ACP allows them to use the pay differently from year to year according to their needs. For example, over the 5-year period we reviewed, the Marine Corps offered the lowest amounts of ACP, ranging from a minimum of $2,000 to a maximum of $20,000. The Air Force and the Army offered the highest levels of ACP, ranging from $12,000 to $25,000; however, despite having the same range, the two services differ on the average bonus amounts awarded, with averages of $20,000 and $15,000 respectively.[30] Each service also determines which of its aviators should receive the highest amounts of bonus based on its determination of an aviation specialty as critical and requiring a bonus. For example, as DOD reported in its 2010 report to Congress on Aviation Continuation Pay,31 in the Air Force's fiscal year 2010 program, the highest amount—$25,000 per year—was offered to pilots who had just completed their undergraduate flying training service commitments and who signed a 5-year agreement. Uncommitted pilots and combat systems officers operating remotely piloted aircraft were offered $15,000 a year for 3-, 4-, or 5-year contracts; air battle managers were offered the same amount for 5-year contracts. By comparison, the Army offered $25,000 per year to Special Operations Aviation Regiment pilots and $12,000 per year to pilots who were Tactical Operations Officers. Each of the services, with the exception of the Army, has decreased the number of servicemembers receiving ACP from fiscal years 2006 to 2010 (see table 2). All services decreased their ACP programs in fiscal year 2010, but each service justified the program as necessary. For example, the Army reported that shortages remained in critical military occupational specialties and incentives were necessary to increase pilot inventories, support present readiness, and enable future transformation. The Air Force stated that the demand for pilots continued to exceed supply. Specifically, it required a large eligibility pool of pilots for remotely piloted aircraft, special operations forces pilots, and air operations center and air liaison officer pilots.

Table 2. Numbers of Servicemembers Who Received Aviation Continuation Pay in Fiscal Years 2006 and 2010

	FY 2006	FY 2010	Percentage change
Army	795	1,208	+34%
Navy	3,127	2,939	-6%
Marine Corps	1,358	1,166	-16%
Air Force	8,562	5,411	-58%

Source: GAO analysis of service data.

In *The Tenth Quadrennial Review of Military Compensation,* DOD identified limited flexibility in managing its special pays as a key weakness in its compensation system.

DOD further stated that some statutory pays were rarely reviewed, updated, or discontinued, even when the staffing concerns they were designed to address had abated.

In order to prevent special and incentive pays from becoming permanent entitlements paid to servicemembers because of statutory requirements, DOD recommended in this review that the more than 60 special and incentive pays be replaced with 8 broad discretionary special and incentive pay authorities that will allow DOD and the services discretion to determine recipients and amounts.

This authority was provided in the National Defense Authorization Act for Fiscal Year 2008 and requires DOD to transition to a consolidated structure over a 10-year period. According to DOD's consolidation plan, the transition will be complete in fiscal year 2014 (see fig. 6). However, OSD officials stated that some pays will be transitioned sooner. For example, OSD is currently preparing a draft policy for transitioning ACP and ACIP, which is expected to be approved this fiscal year by the Secretary of Defense, 1 year ahead of the originally planned date.

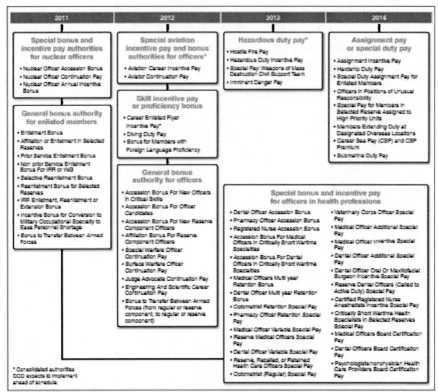

Source: January 2009 Report to Congress on Implementation Plan for Consolidated
    Special and Incentive Pay Authorities by the Office of the Under Secretary of
    Defense for Personnel and Readiness.

Figure 6. DOD's Plan for Consolidating Special and Incentive Pays Into Eight
Categories.

The Tenth Quadrennial Review identified three benefits of consolidating
the statutory authorities for DOD's special and incentive pays. These benefits
include (1) increasing the ability of the services to better target resources to
high priority staffing needs and respond to changing circumstances; (2)
decreasing the number of pays and therefore reducing the administrative
burden of managing over 60 different pays with different sets of rules and
budgets; and (3) increasing performance incentives, by allowing the services
to link some special and incentive pay grades to high performance by
motivating and rewarding effort and achievement. Under the consolidation, for
example, aviator pays will be combined into a single pay authority entitled
"Special Aviation Incentive Pay and Bonus Authorities for Officers," allowing

the services to make payments to aviators depending on staffing needs and other force management issues specific to each service. This consolidation could result in many differences in the ways the services administer these pays. For example, certain aviator occupations may no longer receive an incentive, or incentives could vary by specific occupation or years of service.

DOD has identified perceived benefits of consolidating special and incentive pays, but it does not have baseline metrics in place to measure the effects of its consolidation effort. As we previously reported, organizations should establish baseline measures to assess progress in reaching stated objectives.[32] DOD's January 2009 report on the consolidation effort, the latest such report available, stated that it had only converted a limited number of pays to the new consolidated pay authority, but this report did not outline how effectiveness will be measured for implementing these pays. OSD officials told us that they plan to revise the relevant DOD instructions giving the services guidelines on how to administer the new programs but they did not say these guidelines would include any performance metrics for measuring the effects of the consolidation effort. As a result, DOD may not be positioned to monitor the implementation of this consolidation to determine whether it is in fact resulting in greater flexibility and more precise targeting of resources and what impact the consolidation is having on DOD's budget.

CONCLUSION

From fiscal years 2006 through 2010, the Army's contracted amounts for bonuses rose more dramatically than the other services', as the Army increased its force size and deployed vast numbers of servicemembers to Iraq and Afghanistan. Conversely, the Army was able to more dramatically decrease its bonus contract amounts as the economy declined, the unemployment rate rose, and the Army was not trying to grow its overall force. The Army, and the other services to some extent, demonstrated that they can use bonuses flexibly in response to changing market conditions, but they still do not know whether they are paying more than they need to pay to attract and retain enlisted personnel. Also, at present, DOD has no formal method of facilitating discussions among the services on efficiencies to be gained from assessing the cost-effectiveness of their incentive programs. Although determining optimal bonus amounts is challenging, coordination of research efforts to determine the return on investment of DOD's various programs will become increasingly important as constraints on fiscal resources increase. Moreover, determining optimal bonus amounts will help DOD adjust the amounts for occupations due to changing market conditions. Also, DOD has not yet fully implemented its consolidation authorities, which would give it more flexibility to target its special and incentive pays to those servicemembers it needs most to retain and to discontinue paying some servicemembers these pays when it is no longer necessary to retain them. The statutory requirement to consolidate DOD's more than 60 pays should move DOD toward more flexibility in managing its incentive programs, but it will be critical for DOD to continually monitor its progress toward this goal as it completes the consolidation of its special and incentive pays over the next several years.

RECOMMENDATIONS FOR EXECUTIVE ACTION

We recommend that the Secretary of Defense direct the Under Secretary of Defense for Personnel and Readiness to take the following two actions:

- Coordinate with the services on conducting research, as appropriate, to determine optimal bonus amounts.
- As the consolidation of the special and incentive pay programs is completed over the next 7 years and the instructions directing the services on how to administer the new programs are revised, monitor the implementation of this consolidation to determine whether it is in fact resulting in greater flexibility and more precise targeting of resources and what impact the consolidation is having on DOD's budget.

AGENCY COMMENTS

In written comments on a draft of this report, DOD concurred with both our recommendations. DOD stated that it would find the line of research we discuss in our first recommendation to be beneficial and has discussed this issue on a number of occasions. DOD also said that it will consider this a priority research project and begin it when funds are available. DOD stated that it also agrees, as we discussed in our second recommendation, with the appropriateness of monitoring the implementation of the consolidated authorities to help ensure that they do result in greater flexibility and more precise targeting of resources. However, it stated that, while the department believes that the new authorities will result in more precise targeting of resources, it pointed out that the cost of special and incentive pays could increase or decrease based on market conditions, such as the economy.

Brenda S. Farrell
Director,
Defense Capabilities and Management

APPENDIX I. SCOPE AND METHODOLOGY

This review included an analysis of enlistment and reenlistment bonuses for enlisted personnel, as well as special pays for officers and enlisted personnel in the active components of the Army, the Navy, the Marine Corps, and the Air Force.

We analyzed data on 15 special and incentive pays across the services for fiscal years 2006 through 2010, which represented the top five expenditures for special and incentive pays each year for each service. We focused on pays that were available to most servicemembers. For this reason, we excluded medical pays.

To conduct our work, we analyzed service data on enlistment and reenlistment bonuses, reviewed Department of Defense (DOD) and service regulations related to the use of bonuses and special and incentive pays; interviewed DOD and service officials on the processes and methodological tools in place to identify occupations eligible for bonuses and steps taken to assess the effectiveness of their bonus programs; observed two services' meetings that are convened to determine which occupations should be eligible for bonuses; interviewed researchers knowledgeable about literature on bonus effectiveness; and reviewed selected studies on this subject. We interviewed DOD officials in the Washington, D.C., metropolitan area and conducted a site visit to Millington, Tennessee, to observe the Navy's Working Group convened to determine which occupations should be eligible for bonuses. In the course of our work, we contacted or visited the organizations and offices listed in table 3.

To determine trends in the use of enlistment and reenlistment bonuses, we requested and analyzed service data on enlistment and reenlistment bonuses contracted from fiscal year 2006 through fiscal year 2010. For enlistment bonuses, the services provided data on the amounts contracted for various types of enlistment bonuses that they used for the purpose of attracting individuals into the service, such as bonuses awarded for entering specific occupational specialties, having certain qualifications, or leaving for basic training within a specific amount of time. Some of the bonuses, such as those paid through the Army's Advantage Fund,[1] were only available in some of the years for which the data were requested. In conducting our analyses of enlistment bonuses, we combined the amounts that the services contracted for all enlistment bonuses in a given fiscal year.

Table 3. Organizations and Offices Contacted

Name of organization or office
Army
Office of the Deputy Chief of Staff, Military Personnel Management Directorate
U.S. Army Human Resources Command
U.S. Army Recruiting Command
Navy
Enlisted Personnel Plans and Policy
Economic Analysis and Modeling Division
Community Management
Navy Pay and Compensation
Navy Recruiting Command
Marine Corps
Office of the Deputy Chief of Staff for Manpower and Reserve Affairs
Name of organization or office
Air Force
Enlisted Accessions Policy
Enlistment Force Management
Support and Analysis Branch
Office of the Secretary of Defense
Office of the Under Secretary of Defense for Personnel and Readiness
Office of the Under Secretary of Defense (Comptroller)
Research Organizations
Army Research Institute
Institute for Defense Analyses
Center for Naval Analyses
The Lewin Group
The RAND Corporation

Source: GAO.

For reenlistment bonuses, all services provided data on the amounts contracted in the Selective Reenlistment Bonus (SRB) program, which offers monetary incentives to qualified personnel who reenlist in certain occupations. We assessed the reliability of each service's enlistment and reenlistment bonus data by obtaining information from the services on their systems' ability to record, track, and report on these data, as well as the quality control measures in place to ensure that the data are reliable for reporting purposes. We found enlistment and reenlistment data reported by the services to be sufficiently reliable to demonstrate trends in the services' use of these incentives. In order to observe the trends in the use of enlistment and reenlistment bonuses over time, we adjusted the data provided by the services for inflation by using the Consumer Price Index.

To evaluate the extent to which the services have processes to designate occupations that require bonuses and whether bonus amounts are optimally set, we reviewed DOD and service regulations pertaining to their processes for designating bonus-eligible occupations. We also interviewed relevant officials from the Office of the Secretary of Defense (OSD) and the services with responsibilities for designating occupations as bonus-eligible on the processes in place to determine which occupations should receive bonuses, including the analytical tools such as statistical models used for this purpose. Additionally, we discussed with them how the effectiveness of their bonus programs is measured, requesting any available data to demonstrate the effectiveness of their bonus programs. We also observed two services' meetings that are convened to determine which occupations should be eligible for bonuses.[2]

To determine whether bonus amounts are optimally set, we requested and reviewed the data used by the services to gauge their bonus programs' effectiveness. All the services indicated that they use accession and retention data for that purpose, and we obtained these data for all the services for fiscal years 2006 through 2010 from OSD. In addition, we contacted officials from the Army Research Institute, the Center for Naval Analyses, the Institute for Defense Analyses, RAND, and the Lewin Group to discuss their past and proposed work on bonus effectiveness. We also reviewed selected studies on bonus effectiveness.

To determine how much flexibility DOD has in managing selected special and incentive pays, we requested and analyzed service data on the top five special pays (according to overall expended dollar amount by service) for officer and enlisted active-duty personnel from fiscal year 2006 through fiscal year 2010. The list of the top five pays in each of these years varied by service, as shown in table 4.

Table 4. Selected Top Five Pays for Officer and Enlisted Personnel for Fiscal Years 2006-2010, by Service

	Army	Navy	Marine Corps	Air Force
			Enlisted	
2006	1. Hostile Fire/Imminent Danger Pay	Career Sea Pay	Hostile Fire/Imminent Danger Pay	Hostile Fire/Imminent Danger Pay
	2 Hardship Duty Pay	Special Duty Assignment Pay	Special Duty Assignment Pay	Special Duty Assignment Pay
	3 Special Duty Assignment Pay	Hostile Fire/Imminent Danger Pay	Hardship Duty Pay	Hardship Duty Pay
	4 Parachute Duty Pay	Submarine Duty Incentive Pay	Career Sea Pay	Career Enlisted Flyer Incentive Pay
	5 Foreign Language Proficiency Bonus	Assignment Incentive Pay	Crew Member Flying Duty Pay	Foreign Language Proficiency Bonus
2007	1 Hostile Fire/Imminent Danger Pay	Career Sea Pay	Assignment Incentive Pay	Hostile Fire/Imminent Danger Pay
	2 Hardship Duty Pay	Hostile Fire/Imminent Danger Pay	Hostile Fire/Imminen Danger Pay t	Hardship Duty Pay
	3 Parachute Duty Pay	Special Duty Assignment Pay	Special Duty Assignment Pay	Special Duty Assignment Pay
	4 Special Duty Assignment Pay	Submarine Duty Incentive Pay	Hardship Duty Pay	Career Enlisted Flyer Incentive Pay
	5 Foreign Language Proficiency Bonus	Assignment Incentive Pay	Foreign Language Proficiency Bonus	Foreign Language Proficiency Bonus
2008	1 Hostile Fire/Imminent Danger Pay	Career Sea Pay	Hostile Fire/Imminent Danger Pay	Hostile Fire/Imminent Danger Pay
	2 Hardship Duty Pay	Special Duty Assignment Pay	Special Duty Assignment Pay	Special Duty Assignment Pay
	3 Parachute Duty Pay	Hostile Fire/Imminent Danger Pay	Hardship Duty Pay	Hardship Duty Pay
	4 Special Duty Assignment Pay	Submarine Duty Incentive Pay	Assignment Incentive Pay	Career Enlisted Flyer Incentive Pay
	5 Foreign Language Proficiency Bonus	Assignment Incentive Pay	Foreign Language Proficiency Bonus	Foreign Language Proficiency Bonus
2009	1 Hostile Fire/Imminent Danger Pay	Career Sea Pay	Hostile Fire/Imminent Danger Pay	Hostile Fire/Imminent Danger Pay

	Army	Navy	Marine Corps	Air Force
	2 Hardship Duty Pay	Special Duty Assignment Pay	Special Duty Assignment Pay	Special Duty Assignment Pay
	3 Special Duty Assignment Pay	Hostile Fire/Imminent Danger Pay	Hardship Duty Pay	Hardship Duty Pay
	4 Parachute Duty Pay	Submarine Duty Incentive Pay	Foreign Language Proficiency Bonus	Career Enlisted Flyer Incentive Pay
	5 Foreign Language Proficiency Bonus	Assignment Incentive Pay	Assignment Incentive Pay	Foreign Language Proficiency Bonus
2010	1 Hostile Fire/Imminent Danger Pay	Career Sea Pay	Hostile Fire/Imminent Danger Pay	Hostile Fire/Imminent Danger Pay
	2 Hardship Duty Pay	Special Duty Assignment Pay	Special Duty Assignment Pay	Hardship Duty Pay
	3 Special Duty Assignment Pay	Hostile Fire/Imminent Danger Pay	Hardship Duty Pay	Special Duty Assignment Pay
	4 Parachute Duty Pay	Submarine Duty Incentive Pay	Foreign Language Proficiency Bonus	Career Enlisted Flyer Incentive Pay
	5 Foreign Language Proficiency Bonus	Assignment Incentive Pay	Career Sea Pay	Assignment Incentive Pay
			Officer	
	Army	Navy	Marine Corps	Air Force
2006	1 Hostile Fire/Imminent Danger Pay	Aviation Career Incentive Pay	Aviation Career Incentive Pay	Aviation Continuation Pay
	2 Aviation Career Incentive Pay	Submarine Duty Incentive Pay	Aviation Continuation Pay	Aviation Career Incentive Pay
	3 Hardship Duty Pay	Aviation Continuation Pay	Hostile Fire/Imminent Danger Pay	Critical Skills Retention Bonus
	4 Parachute Duty Pay	Nuclear Officer Incentive Pay	Hardship Duty Pay	Hostile Fire/Imminent Danger Pay
	5 Aviation Continuation Pay	Career Sea Pay	Career Sea Pay	Hardship Duty Pay
2007	1 Aviation Career Incentive Pay	Aviation Career Incentive Pay	Aviation Career Incentive Pay	Aviation Continuation Pay
	2 Hostile Fire/Imminent Danger Pay	Nuclear Officer Incentive Pay	Aviation Continuation Pay	Aviation Career Incentive Pay

Table 4. (Continued)

	Army	Navy	Marine Corps	Air Force
	3 Hardship Duty Pay	Aviation Continuation Pay	Hostile Fire/Imminent Danger Pay	Hostile Fire/Imminent Danger Pay
	4 Aviation Continuation Pay	Submarine Duty Incentive	Hardship Duty Pay	Foreign Language Proficiency Bonus
	5 Parachute Duty Pay	Career Sea Pay	Foreign Language Proficiency Bonus	Hardship Duty Pay
2008	1 Critical Skills Retention Bonus	Aviation Career Incentive Pay	Aviation Career Incentive Pay	Aviation Continuation Pay
	2 Hostile Fire/Imminent Danger	Aviation Continuation Pay	Aviation Continuation Pay	Aviation Career Incentive Pay
	3 Aviation Career Incentive Pay	Nuclear Officer Incentive Pay	Hostile Fire/Imminent	Hostile Fire/Imminent
	4 Hardship Duty Pay	Submarine Duty Incentive Pay	Hardship Duty Pay	Hardship Duty Pay
	5 Critical Skills Retention Bonus	Career Sea Pay	Foreign Language Proficiency Bonus	Foreign Language Proficiency Bonus
2009	1 Hostile Fire/Imminent Danger	Aviation Career Incentive Pay	Aviation Career Incentive Pay	Aviation Career Incentive Pay
	2 Aviation Career Incentive Pay	Nuclear Officer Incentive Pay	Aviation Continuation Pay	Aviation Continuation Pay
	3 Hardship Duty Pay	Aviation Continuation Pay	Hostile Fire/Imminent	Hostile Fire/Imminent
	4 Critical Skills Retention Bonus	Submarine Duty Incentive Pay	Critical Skills Retention Bonus	Critical Skills Retention Bonus
	5 Crew Member Flying Duty Pay	Career Sea Pay	Hardship Duty Pay	Hardship Duty Pay
2010	1 Hostile Fire/Imminent Danger	Aviation Career Incentive Pay	Aviation Career Incentive Pay	Aviation Career Incentive Pay
	2 Aviation Career Incentive Pay	Nuclear Officer Incentive Pay	Aviation Continuation Pay	Aviation Continuation Pay
	3 Hardship Duty Pay	Aviation Continuation Pay	Hostile Fire/Imminent	Hostile Fire/Imminent
	4 Aviation Continuation Pay	Submarine Duty Incentive Pay	Hardship Duty Pay	Hardship Duty Pay
	Judge Advocate 5 Continuation Pay	Career Sea Pay	Foreign Language Proficiency Bonus	Foreign Language Proficiency Bonus

Source: GAO analysis of service data.

For the purposes of this objective, we excluded enlistment and selective reenlistment bonuses because we addressed them in detail in previous objectives. We also excluded the Critical Skills Retention Bonus for enlisted personnel. In addition, we excluded medical pays for enlisted personnel and officers because we focused on pays that were available to most servicemembers.

We assessed the reliability of each service's special pays data by obtaining information from the services on their systems' ability to record, track, and report on these data, as well as the quality control measures in place to ensure that the data are reliable for reporting purposes. We found the special pays data reported by the services to be sufficiently reliable for demonstrating trends in the services' use of these incentives over time.

In addition, we interviewed DOD officials on their role in managing special pay programs, the amount of flexibility they have over them, and their ongoing efforts to consolidate these pays. We also requested and reviewed DOD reports and other documents pertaining to special pays and the consolidation effort, such as the 2010 report to Congress on Aviation Continuation Pay and the 2009 report to Congress on the implementation plan for the consolidation of special pays.

We conducted this performance audit from September 2010 through June 2011 in accordance with generally accepted government auditing standards. These standards require that we plan and perform the audit to obtain sufficient, appropriate evidence to provide a reasonable basis for our findings and conclusions based on our research objectives. We believe that the evidence obtained provides a reasonable basis for our findings and conclusions based on our audit objectives.

End Notes

[1] DOD has over 60 special and incentive pays across the services that provide compensation for skill sets, such as foreign language proficiency, as well as occupations, such as aviation and medical professions. In addition, DOD also offers bonuses specifically for recruitment and retention.

[2] For more information on servicemembers' compensation, see GAO, Military Personnel: Military and Civilian Pay Comparisons Present Challenges and Are One of Many Tools in Assessing Compensation, GAO-10-561R (Washington, D.C.: Apr.1, 2010).

[3] GAO, Military Personnel: DOD Needs to Improve the Transparency and Reassess the Reasonableness, Appropriateness, Affordability, and Sustainability of Its Military Compensation System, GAO-05-798 (Washington, D.C.: July 19, 2005).

[4] S. Rep. No. 111-201, at 145 (2010).

[5] The Secretary of Defense Memorandum, Track Four Efficiency Initiative Decisions (Mar. 14, 2011) emphasizes areas of efficiency that reduce duplication, overhead, and excess.

[6] Office of the Under Secretary of Defense, Department of Defense, Report of the Tenth Quadrennial Review of Military Compensation, Volume I: Cash Compensation (Washington, D.C.: February 2008).

[7] DOD Directive 1304.21, Policy on Enlistment Bonuses, Accession Bonuses for New Officers in Critical Skills, Selective Reenlistment Bonuses, and Critical Skills Retention Bonuses for Active Members (Jan. 31, 2005).

[8] GAO, Military Personnel: Military and Civilian Pay Comparisons Present Challenges and Are One of Many Tools in Assessing Compensation, GAO-10-561R (Washington, D.C.: Apr. 1, 2010).

[9] GAO, Military Personnel: Army Needs to Focus on Cost-Effective Use of Financial Incentives and Quality Standards in Managing Growth, GAO-09-256 (Washington, D.C.: May 4, 2009).

[10] These figures reflect the total amounts of contracts signed by enlistees or reenlistees. Persons who reenlist may receive their bonuses shortly after signing their contracts, but new enlistees must complete training in the assigned occupation or meet other qualifications listed in the contract before they receive their bonuses. As such, the "contracted amounts" may not reflect actual amounts paid in that fiscal year.

[11] Historically, DOD has used two primary measures to identify quality recruits: possession of a high-school diploma and a score in the upper half on the Armed Forces Qualification Test (AFQT). DOD's goals for the services are that at least 90 percent of recruits each year have a high-school diploma, at least 60 percent score in the upper half on the AFQT, and no more than 4 percent score in the bottom 30 percent on the AFQT.

[12] The Navy met 96 percent of its goal in fiscal year 2006. The Air Force met 97 percent of its goal in fiscal year 2007, 72 percent in fiscal year 2008, and 98 percent in fiscal year 2010. The Marine Corps met 95 percent of its goal in fiscal year 2008.

[13] Sections 308 and 309 of Title 37 of the U.S. Code provide that enlistment or reenlistment bonuses may be paid to eligible individuals. These enlistment bonuses and reenlistment bonuses are discretionary pays in that they are not required by law to be paid to every eligible individual.

[14] We did not independently assess the validity of the models used by the services. In July 2010, we reported on the services' processes, including their models, for determining requirements for medical personnel to staff military treatment facilities. We stated that the services' processes were not, in all cases, validated and verifiable, as DOD policy requires. We recommended that the services take actions to improve their medical requirements determination processes. DOD generally concurred with our recommendations and cited actions it planned to take in response. See GAO, Military Personnel: Enhanced Collaboration and Process Improvements Needed for Determining Military Treatment Facility Medical Personnel Requirements, GAO-10-696 (Washington, D.C.: July 29, 2010).

[15] Department of Defense Directive 1304.21, Policy on Enlistment Bonuses, Accession Bonuses for New Officers in Critical Skills, Selective Reenlistment Bonuses, and Critical Skills Retention Bonuses for Active Members (Jan. 31, 2005) and Department of Defense Instruction 1304.29, Administration of Enlistment Bonuses, Accession Bonuses for New Officers in Critical Skills, Selective Reenlistment Bonuses, and Critical Skills Retention Bonuses for Active Members (Dec. 15, 2004).

[16] When making enlistment bonus decisions, the Army places occupations into specific categories, or levels. Currently, the Army has five levels that qualify for an incentive.

Enlistees entering occupations in levels 1 through 4 receive a cash bonus of varying amounts, depending on length of enlistment. Enlistees entering level 5 occupations are eligible for educational loan repayment but not a cash bonus. The dollar amounts associated with each level are adjusted periodically, but Army officials interviewed said that these adjustments are not made frequently. Participants in the quarterly Enlisted Incentives Review Boards do not offer input into specific bonus amounts; they instead focus on assigning occupational specialties to one of these levels.

[17] DOD Directive 1304.21, Policy on Enlistment Bonuses, Accession Bonuses for New Officers in Critical Skills, Selective Reenlistment Bonuses, and Critical Skills Retention Bonuses for Active Members (Jan. 31, 2005). Department of Defense Instruction 1304.29, Administration of Enlistment Bonuses, Accession Bonuses for New Officers in Critical Skills, Selective Reenlistment Bonuses, and Critical Skills Retention Bonuses for Active Members (Dec. 15, 2004).

[18] The Military Compensation System: Completing the Transition to an All-Volunteer Force (Arlington, Va: Apr. 28, 2006).

[19] RAND, The Enlistment Bonus Experiment (1986).

[20] DOD reported that it is in the process of analyzing the effectiveness of special and incentive pays for Special Operations Forces and the efficiencies in the incentive pays approval process. DOD is also developing a model for analyzing the effectiveness of special and incentive pays for officers and is in the process of identifying a contractor for this work. According to DOD, these studies focus on the effectiveness and efficiency of special and incentive pays generally for specific groups of military personnel.

[21] GAO, Military Draft: Potential Impacts and Other Issues, GAO/NSIAD-88-102 (Washington, D.C.: Mar. 10, 1988).

[22] GAO, Military Personnel: Army Needs to Focus on Cost-Effective Use of Financial Incentives and Quality Standards in Managing Force Growth, GAO-09-256 (Washington, D.C.: May 4, 2009).

[23] RAND, Cash Incentives and Military Enlistment, Attrition, and Reenlistment (2010). RAND found that the increase in enlistment bonuses that occurred in the Army from October 2004 to September 2008 increased high-quality enlistments and that, in the absence of this increase, the Army would not have been able to meet its recruiting goals during that time period. RAND also found that eliminating the Selective Reenlistment Bonus program would have reduced the rate of reenlistment in the Army and the Marine Corps, although the effects for the Navy and the Air Force were more modest.

[24] We did not independently review these methodologies and did not assess the extent to which they will be effective in providing DOD and the services with information on the most cost-effective bonus amounts.

[25] An econometric study involves the statistical analysis of historical data to assess the independent effect of bonuses on recruiting and retention while controlling for, or holding constant, other external factors that may affect recruiting and retention.

[26] An experiment would involve the random assignment of individuals to groups receiving different amounts of bonuses and following their recruiting and retention outcomes, while also controlling for other factors that may affect these outcomes.

[27] Pub. L. No. 110-181, §§ 661 and 662.

[28] For our review, we included 15 special and incentive pays that represented the top five categories for each service (excluding medical pays, enlistment, selective reenlistment, and critical skills retention bonuses) during fiscal years 2006 through 2010. They are the following: Assignment Incentive Pay, Aviation Continuation Pay, Aviation Career

Incentive Pay, Career Enlisted Flyer Incentive Pay, Career Sea Pay, Critical Skills Retention Bonus, Foreign Language Proficiency Bonus, Hardship Duty Pay, Hostile Fire/Imminent Danger Pay, Judge Advocate Continuation Pay, Nuclear Officer Incentive Pay, Special Duty Assignment Pay, Submarine Duty Incentive Pay, Crew Member Flying Duty Pay, and Parachute Duty Pay (the previous two pays are a subset of Hazardous Duty Pay).

29 An officer who is entitled to basic pay, holds an aeronautical rating or designation, and is qualified for aviation service under regulations prescribed by the Secretary of Defense, among other requirements, is entitled to continuous monthly incentive pay.

30 The Army data reported are based on fiscal years 2006, 2007, and 2010 because these were the only years in which ACP expenditures made the selected top five special and incentive pay list.

31 DOD, Report to Congress, Aviation Continuation Pay (ACP) Programs for Fiscal Year 2010 (March 2011). This annual report is required by U.S. Code, title 37, § 301b(i) and is to be submitted to the Senate and House Committees on Armed Services.

32 GAO, Standards for Internal Control in the Federal Government, GAO/AIMD-00-21.3.1 (Washington, D.C.: November 1999) and Executive Guide: Effectively Implementing the Government Performance and Results Act, GAO/GGD-96-118 (Washington, D.C.: June 1996).

End notes for Appendix I

[1] The Army Advantage Fund (AAF) was created under the authority provided by section 681 of the National Defense Authorization Act for Fiscal Year 2006 (Pub. L. No. 109-163 (2006)) to encourage potential candidates to join the Army by giving them money toward a down payment or mortgage on a home or the development of a small business. The AAF Pilot Program was an incentive intended to give the Army a competitive advantage in attracting eligible high-quality individuals who otherwise would not have considered the Army as a career. The AAF was suspended in February 2009 due to favorable changes in recruiting conditions and requirements that no longer necessitated the use of the AAF for market expansion.

[2] We observed the Army's Enlisted Incentives Review Board in December 2010 and a portion of the Navy's Working Group in February 2011.

In: Military Pay and Benefits
Editor: Walter Avraham

ISBN: 978-1-62417-809-2
© 2013 Nova Science Publishers, Inc.

Chapter 4

Evaluating Military Compensation. Statement of Carla Tighe Murray, Senior Analyst for Military Compensation and Health Care, Congressional Budget Office. Hearing on "Military Compensation and Benefits"[*]

Mr. Chairman, Senator Graham, and Members of the Subcommittee, I appreciate the opportunity to discuss the Congressional Budget Office's (CBO's) analysis of compensation for members of the armed forces. To attract and retain the military personnel it needs, the Department of Defense (DoD) must offer a competitive compensation package—one that adequately rewards service members for their training and skills as well as for the rigors of military life, particularly the prospect of wartime deployment.

The best barometer of the effectiveness of DoD's compensation system may be how well the military attracts and retains high-quality personnel. Between 2005 and 2008, the services periodically had trouble recruiting or retaining all of the high-quality personnel they needed.[1] To address those problems, the Congress authorized increases in both cash compensation (such as pay raises and bonuses) and noncash compensation (such as expanded

---

[*] This is an edited, reformatted and augmented version of a Statement Presented April 28, 2010 before the Senate Armed Services Committee, Subcommittee on Personnel.

education benefits for veterans and their families). All of the services met their recruiting and retention goals in 2009 and are continuing to do so in 2010. However, the relationship between specific changes in pay rates and benefits and the amount of recruiting and retention is not clear, and changes in recruiting and retention may be too gradual or too ambiguous to guide all decisions about compensation. In particular, a variety of factors—including economic conditions—may have significant effects on DoD's ability to recruit and retain personnel during a given period. Therefore, it is difficult to determine the appropriate increase in compensation solely on the basis of recent patterns of recruiting and retention.

Even when overall goals for recruiting and retention are met, shortages or surpluses may exist in specific occupations or among people with certain years of service or rank. In those cases, the military services have other tools at their disposal. For example, they can enhance their efforts to attract recruits and can fine-tune their bonus programs to retain existing personnel who possess particular occupational skills.

Another way to determine whether military compensation is competitive is to compare it with civilian compensation. This testimony will focus primarily on such comparisons—which can be useful but not definitive, in part because of the significant differences in working conditions and benefits between military and civilian jobs.

My remarks today will address three questions:

- *How does military cash compensation compare with civilian wages and salaries?* CBO's most recent analysis, for calendar year 2006, found that average cash compensation for service members (including tax-free cash allowances for housing and food) was greater than that of more than 75 percent of civilians of comparable age and educational achievement. Since then, military pay raises have continued to exceed the increases of civilian wages and salaries, so that finding has not changed.

- *Is there a "gap" between civilian and military pay raises over the past few decades?* The answer depends on how narrowly military cash pay is defined. One common method of comparison is to calculate the cumulative difference between increases in military and civilian pay using military basic pay, a narrow measure of cash compensation that does not include, for example, tax-free allowances for housing and food. Applying that method would indicate that cumulatively, civilian pay rose by about 2 percent more than military pay between 1982 and the beginning of 2010. But that measure does not encompass the full scope of military cash compensation. Using a broader measure that includes cash allowances for housing and food indicates that the cumulative increase in military compensation has *exceeded* the cumulative increase in private-sector wages and salaries by 11 percent since 1982. That comparison excludes the value of noncash and deferred benefits, which would probably add to the cumulative difference, because benefits such as military health care have expanded more rapidly than corresponding benefits in the private sector.

- *How would the costs of using bonuses to enhance recruiting and retention compare with the costs of adding more to basic pay?* Traditionally, service members receive an across-the-board increase in basic pay each calendar year, and proposals are frequently made to boost the rate of increase. Changing the basic-pay raise that will take effect on January 1, 2011, from the 1.4 percent requested by the President and DoD to 1.9 percent, for example, would increase DoD's costs by about $350 million in 2011 and by a total of about $2.4 billion through 2015, CBO estimates. A larger pay raise would probably enhance recruiting and retention, although the effect would be small. One possible alternative would be to increase cash bonuses by enough to achieve the same recruiting and retention effects as a higher across-the-board pay raise. That approach would have a smaller impact on DoD's costs because bonuses can be awarded only to the types of service members the military needs most. Bonuses can also be focused on current personnel or potential enlistees who are at the point of making career decisions. Unlike pay raises, bonuses do not compound from year to year (a higher pay raise in one year will cause the following year's raise to be applied to a higher base), and bonuses do not affect retirement pay and other elements of compensation.

THE STRUCTURE OF MILITARY COMPENSATION

Earnings can be measured in several different ways, but most studies begin with cash compensation. For the military, the narrowest measure of cash compensation is basic pay. All members of the armed services on active duty receive basic pay, which varies according to rank and years of service. A broader measure of cash compensation— called regular military compensation (RMC)—consists of basic pay plus service members' basic allowances for housing and subsistence, as well as the tax advantage that arises because those allowances are not subject to federal income taxes. All personnel are entitled to receive RMC, and DoD has used it as a fundamental measure of military pay since at least 1962.[2]

While on active duty, service members may also receive various types of special pay, incentive pay, bonuses, and allowances that are not counted in RMC. Those cash payments help compensate service members for unique features of military life. They may be awarded to personnel who possess particular skills or undertake hazardous duty, including deployment and combat. Personnel may also earn bonus payments when they reenlist after completing their contracted term of service, especially if they have occupational skills that are in short supply. Because those special types of pay are earned irregularly or by a small number of specialists, they are generally excluded when comparing military and civilian compensation.

The broadest measure of military compensation includes noncash or deferred benefits, such as retirement pay, health care, and veterans' benefits. In both the armed forces and civilian jobs, such benefits can be sizable and can influence people's decisions about employment, including whether to enlist or reenlist in the military. Non-cash benefits make up about half of total compensation for the average service member, CBO estimates—compared with about one-third for the average civilian worker. Thus, a measure of compensation that includes all noncash and deferred benefits gives a broader and clearer picture of the military's entire compensation package and provides a useful framework for analyzing service members' cash compensation. However, such a comprehensive measure combines funds in different defense appropriation titles and in departments other than DoD; thus, it is more difficult to use than narrower measures of cash compensation to assess a particular department's budget.

HOW DOES MILITARY PAY COMPARE WITH CIVILIAN PAY?

The results of pay comparisons differ depending on the definition of military compensation and the segment of the civilian population used in the comparison. Most enlisted personnel join the military soon after high school, but they generally receive some college-level education while on active duty.

(The share of enlisted personnel with at least one year of college education grew from 32 percent in 1985 to 72 percent in 2005, CBO estimates.) DoD has asserted that in order to keep experienced personnel in the force, military pay must compare favorably with the wages of college-educated civilians rather than high school graduates. Specifically, DoD's goal has been to make RMC comparable with the 70th percentile of earnings for civilians who have some college education.[3]

CBO estimated that in calendar year 2006, average basic pay for enlisted personnel closely matched the 50th percentile of estimated earnings for civilians with some college education—in other words, roughly half of those civilians had earnings that were higher than average basic pay and half had earnings that were lower.[4] CBO also estimated that average RMC (which includes cash allowances and associated tax advantages) exceeded the 75th percentile of earnings for civilians with some college education, surpassing DoD's goal. Lawmakers have continued to authorize military pay raises that exceed the average rise in civilian wages and salaries, so those measures of military compensation would probably match higher percentiles of civilian earnings today. CBO's study also concluded that service members have access to a range of benefits not routinely offered in the private sector, including free or low-cost health care, housing, education assistance, and discount shopping. Other studies of cash and noncash compensation have reached similar conclusions.[5]

Comparisons of military and civilian pay have several important limitations. First, working conditions can differ markedly between military and civilian jobs. For example, military personnel are generally expected to change locations every few years—in addition to deploying for specific operations—whereas most civilians can choose to remain in the same area throughout their career. Military personnel may work longer hours or in more hazardous conditions than civilians do, even if their type of occupation is the same. At the same time, military life includes features that people may find more attractive than comparable civilian jobs. Some military personnel receive greater responsibility earlier in their career than civilians do. Job security and group solidarity can also be greater for military personnel than for civilians. Pay comparisons cannot easily incorporate those intangible job characteristics.

Second, pay comparisons may ignore the value of training and education that are provided on the job. DoD generally tries to enlist capable young people with high school diplomas or some college education and then trains them for military life and for their occupational specialty. Civilian employers, by contrast, generally hire people who have already been trained, often at their own expense (although most large employers offer work-related education assistance). In addition, civilian employers are more likely to hire people who have more experience. Adding in the value of government-provided training and education would generally make the noncash share of total military compensation even greater relative to civilian compensation.

Third, differences between military and civilian career patterns complicate pay comparisons. Because the military "promotes from within," pay may need to be higher for new recruits than for civilians of similar ages and education levels as DoD tries to compete for the best pool of applicants from which to select the best career personnel. Also, data on average civilian compensation include the pay of people who are successful in their civilian career as well as the pay of people who are not. But in the military, the "up-or-out" promotion system means that the least successful personnel have generally left military service before reaching senior levels.

Is There a "Gap" Between Military and Civilian Pay Raises?

Because basic pay makes up the majority of regular military compensation, one of the most common comparisons is between changes in military basic pay and changes in the employment cost index (ECI) for wages and salaries of private-sector workers. In 1981 and 1982, relatively large increases in basic pay were enacted to address shortfalls in recruiting and retention. For much of the following two decades, however, basic pay increased more slowly than the ECI did. Some observers have measured the percentage by which the cumulative increase in military basic pay since 1982 has fallen short of the cumulative increase in the ECI for private-sector wages and salaries, referring to that difference as a military "pay gap." By 1998, the gap totaled nearly 14 percent (see Figure 1).

Lawmakers enacted several measures that helped narrow the perceived gap. In November 2003, for example, they passed a provision stipulating that the increases in basic pay for 2004, 2005, and 2006 exceed the corresponding increases in the ECI by 0.5 percentage points.[6] Each year since then, the Congress has continued to set the basic-pay raise at 0.5 percentage points above the increase in the ECI.[7] As a result, the cumulative difference between increases in basic pay and the ECI since 1982 has shrunk to a little over 2 percent.

As a basis for evaluating pay, however, the gap between military and civilian raises since 1982 has some significant limitations.[8] First, the ECI is based on a survey that includes a broad sample of civilian workers; on average, those workers are older than military personnel and more likely to have college degrees. Since 1980, the pay of college-educated workers has risen faster than that of high school graduates in the civilian sector. Also, the pay of older civilian workers has generally grown faster than that of younger workers. Because the military mainly recruits young high school graduates, pay raises that were smaller than increases in the ECI would not necessarily hamper DoD's efforts to attract new personnel.

Second, the pay-gap calculation focuses on one part of military compensation—basic pay—and ignores changes in other cash and noncash components. In 2000, besides raising basic pay, lawmakers authorized a restructuring of housing allowances that eliminated out-of-pocket expenses typically paid by service members (which had averaged about 20 percent of housing costs).[9] Other changes included linking housing allowances more closely to increases in local housing prices and giving service members "rate protection" from any declines in those prices.

With RMC substituted for basic pay in the comparison, the total growth in military compensation since 1982 has exceeded the growth in the ECI for private-sector wages and salaries by about 11 percent (see Figure 1). Including the value of noncash and deferred benefits would probably add to that cumulative difference.

WHAT ARE THE EFFECTS OF CHANGING BASIC PAY VERSUS AWARDING HIGHER BONUSES?

Increasing basic pay in 2011 will affect DoD's budgetary requirements in future years. Pay raises compound from one year to the next, because a higher raise this year will cause next year's rate of increase to be applied to a higher base. Changes in basic pay also affect other components of compensation, such as retirement pay. CBO estimates that increasing the basic-pay raise that will take effect on January 1, 2011, from 1.4 percent, as requested by DoD and the President, to 1.9 percent would boost DoD's personnel costs by about $350 million in 2011 as well as by a total of about $2 billion over the following four years (see Table 1).

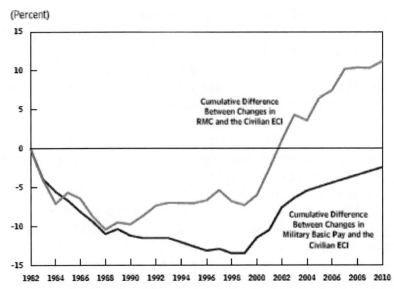

(Percent)

Source: Congressional Budget Office based on data from the Department of Defense
  and the Department of Labor.

Notes: RMC = regular military compensation (basic pay, cash allowances for housing
  and subsistence, and the federal tax advantage that occurs because those
  allowances are not taxed); ECI = employment cost index for wages and salaries in
  private industry.

These comparisons exclude noncash benefits and the military's various types of special
  pay and bonuses.

Figure 1. Difference Between Changes in Military and Civilian Compensation Since
1982.

A higher pay raise would most likely enhance recruiting and retention, but
the effect would be small. The annual difference between a 1.4 percent
increase and a 1.9 percent increase in basic pay for the average enlisted
member is about $150. CBO estimates that roughly 1,000 people who would
not choose to enlist or reenlist in 2011 if basic pay rose by 1.4 percent would
do so with the higher raise.

Alternatively, the same result might be accomplished by increasing
bonuses for enlistment and reenlistment or by stepping up recruiting efforts. A
bonus program generally requires smaller increases in spending than a basic-
pay raise does to achieve the same effect on recruiting and retention, for
several reasons. Bonuses can be targeted toward those service members (or
potential recruits) whom the military needs most. Bonuses do not compound,
as pay raises do, and they do not affect retirement pay and other elements of

compensation. Bonuses also do not involve expending resources on service members who do not have the option of leaving in a particular year; they can be focused on the years of service in which personnel make career decisions and can be curtailed if other factors (such as economic conditions or deployment requirements) change. In addition, larger bonuses could create more-meaningful differences in pay between occupations, which could be a cost-effective tool for improving military readiness.

However, amplifying pay differences between occupations or between people at slightly different stages of their career could run counter to the long-standing principle of military compensation that personnel with similar amounts of responsibility should receive similar pay. Also, increasing bonuses rather than adding to basic pay would reduce retirement and other benefits for service members relative to what they would receive if the extra money was part of basic pay throughout their career.

Table 1. Costs to DoD of Increasing the Basic-Pay Raise from 1.4 Percent to 1.9 Percent in 2011 (By fiscal year, in millions of dollars)

	2011	2012	2013	2014	2015	2016	2017	2018	2019	2020	Total 2011-2015	Total 2011-2020
Budget Authority	367	495	502	511	524	538	554	571	588	606	2,399	5,256
Outlays	348	488	501	510	523	537	553	570	587	604	2,370	5,221

Source: Congressional Budget Office based on data from the Department of Defense (DoD).

Note: Although the numbers shown here are for fiscal years, military pay raises generally take effect on January 1 (the beginning of the second quarter of the fiscal year). These numbers apply to active-duty and reserve personnel but not to members of the Coast Guard or other branches of the uniformed services.

How much it would cost to attract and retain the same number of personnel with bonuses rather than a larger increase in basic pay would depend on how the services structured their bonus programs. In any event, the lack of compounding means that in 2012 and beyond, virtually all service members would have lower overall compensation than they would receive with a larger increase in basic pay. That outcome could also affect recruiting and retention in future years. If DoD wanted to attain the same levels of recruiting and retention as it would achieve with the higher basic pay, an augmented bonus program would need to continue in future years as well.

End Notes

[1] Congressional Budget Office, Recruiting, Retention, and Future Levels of Military Personnel (October 2006). Data for later years come from DoD's Directorate for Accession Policy and Directorate for Officer and Enlisted Personnel Management.

[2] Department of Defense, Under Secretary of Defense for Personnel and Readiness, Report of the 9th Quadrennial Review of Military Compensation, vol. 1 (March 2002), p. 29.

[3] Ibid. Two years ago, DoD's 10th Quadrennial Review of Military Compensation developed a new measure of compensation—called military annual compensation (MAC)—that would include selected noncash elements and deferred compensation. The review's authors recommended making MAC comparable to the 80th percentile of civilian earnings (including similar noncash elements). DoD has not adopted the new measure and continues to use RMC; see, for example, the statement of Clifford L. Stanley, Under Secretary of Defense for Personnel and Readiness, before the Subcommittee on Personnel, Senate Armed Services Committee, March 10, 2010.

[4] Congressional Budget Office, Evaluating Military Compensation (June 2007).

[5] See Department of Defense, Under Secretary of Defense for Personnel and Readiness, Report of the 10th Quadrennial Review of Military Compensation, vol. 1 (February 2008); James E. Grefer, Comparing Military and Civilian Compensation Packages (Alexandria, Va.: CNA, March 2008); Government Accountability Office, Military Personnel: DoD Needs to Improve the Transparency and Reassess the Reasonableness, Appropriateness, Affordability, and Sustainability of Its Military Compensation System, GAO-05-798 (July 2005); Beth J. Asch, James Hosek, and Craig Martin, A Look at Cash Compensation for Active-Duty Military Personnel, MR-1492-OSD (Santa Monica, Calif.: RAND Corporation, 2002); and Congressional Budget Office, Military Compensation: Balancing Cash and Noncash Benefits, Issue Brief (January 16, 2004).

[6] Section 602 of the National Defense Authorization Act for Fiscal Year 2004 (117 Stat. 1498, 37 U.S.C. 1009).

[7] For example, the President requested a 2.9 percent increase in basic pay for 2010, which equaled the percentage increase in the ECI. The Congress authorized a 3.4 percent pay raise in section 601 of the National Defense

[8] Authorization Act for Fiscal Year 2010 (123 Stat. 2347, 37 U.S.C. 1009). CBO produced a technical analysis of those limitations in 1999, and they continue to exist today. See Congressional Budget Office, What Does the Military "Pay Gap" Mean? (June 1999).

[9] Those changes were enacted in section 605 of the National Defense Authorization Act for Fiscal Year 2001 (114 Stat. 1654A-147, 37 U.S.C. 403).

INDEX